Organizational Alpha

BEN CARLSON

ISBN-10: 1541043677
ISBN-13: 978-1541043671

CONTENTS

Introduction: Vision & Details   1

1   Goals-Based Investing   5

2   Defining Your Role as a Fiduciary   9

3   The Decision-Making Process   14

4   The Investment Process   26

5   Choosing an Outsourced Consultant or Advisor   38

6   Alternative Investments   48

7   Investment Policy   64

Conclusion: Creating Organizational Alpha   77

INTRODUCTION: VISION & DETAILS

I've spent my entire career managing institutional portfolios so I'm often asked for recommendations on the best books to read on the subject. There's really only one. Without question that book is *Pioneering Portfolio Management: An Unconventional Approach to Institutional Investment* by Yale's David Swensen. This is the bible for many institutional investors; but that's really it, as far as it goes for books, in this space.

While Swensen's book is certainly chock full of useful advice on how to run a successful investment program, many readers have probably taken away the wrong message after reading it; namely, that they can match Swensen's success and imitate his spectacular results.

Over the past three decades, the Yale Endowment has grown at a rate of roughly 14 percent per year. The fund now has around $26 billion under management. In that time, they've outperformed the average college endowment fund by 5 percent per year. Institutions trying to emulate Swensen's success are akin to individuals trying to copycat Warren Buffett's investment success - it's never going to happen.

What Swensen has achieved with his performance is known in the investing world as alpha. Alpha is a fancy mathematical output that gauges investment performance against a market or an index, after adjusting for risk. In other words, investment alpha is risk-adjusted outperformance. The problem is that investment alpha is a finite resource and can be fleeting. In fact, seeking alpha can often lead to worse results over time for investors who don't possess the skills, resources or discipline necessary to achieve it. Organizational alpha is something that every individual or firm can adopt to add value through intelligent planning, cultivating the right type of culture, creating a thorough decision-making process and understanding who they are (strengths, limitations, investing acumen, etc.).

It makes sense that other nonprofits and institutions would try to follow a similar approach, but it's not so easy. Not only was Swensen a pioneer in his portfolio management techniques - which include a heavy equity bias in illiquid asset classes - but most organizations don't have the knowhow, skill or organizational structure in place to attempt it in the first place.

The "Yale's" of the world get all of the press, but there are a surprisingly large number of smaller nonprofit funds in the United States. According to the IRS, there are close to 80,000 private foundations in the U.S. Roughly 99 percent of these charitable funds have assets of less than $100 million in financial assets. According to the National Association of College and University Business Officers (NACUBO), there are more than 800 universities with an endowment fund, and only ninety-five or so have more than $1 billion. And that's not to mention the trillions of dollars in municipal and private pension plans across the country. In all, it's estimated that there is over $75 trillion managed by institutional investors in the U.S. alone.

Because it's likely that only 1 percent or so of these funds can realistically expect to follow the David Swensen approach to asset management, I decided to write this book to help the other 99 percent of organizations make better decisions with their investment programs.

The goal of this book is to provide a roadmap for those nonprofits and institutional investors who need help managing their money or understanding what really matters when making financial decisions. There is no shortage of bad advice floating around, making it difficult to focus on those areas in an investment program that truly can make a difference and add value in an effort to achieve an organization's goals.

In the finance industry people tend to focus on the large amounts of money that these institutions have, but they forget about the important missions these funds are tasked with. The U.S. is actually fairly unique in terms of how charitable its citizens are. Those 80,000-plus foundations are doing great work in a number of different areas - health care, research, education, scholarships, food, children and the underprivileged, to name a few. And pension plans are invested to help private sector and government employees enjoy a secure retirement. This money is there to make a difference, not entertain people on Wall Street.

Most small and mid-sized nonprofits can have a huge impact on their communities with the work they perform, but a lack of financial resources can often cause strains on their business models. There has probably never been more competition for charitable donations than there is today. The number of charities continues to grow, which is a wonderful thing; but Federal funding for these organizations has begun to wane. Ivy League schools and many of the largest charities have a near endless supply of wealthy donors at their disposal, while small and mid-sized institutions and funds have to fight for every dollar in contributions. Investments may have to pick up more (or even all) of the slack in some cases to meet annual spending needs. It can be difficult to find qualified staff to run a portfolio when you don't have the billions of dollars at your disposal. The leaders of these nonprofits are rightfully more worried about running their organization than managing their portfolios.

INDIVIDUALS VERSUS INSTITUTIONS

Institutional funds are often labeled "sophisticated" because they control larger pools of capital, leading many to assume there's a need to make things overly complicated. It took me some time to come to this realization, but from a portfolio management perspective, more money just means a few more zeroes. Complex problems don't always require complex solutions.

Whether you're an individual with a small brokerage account or a multi-billion-dollar pension plan, you still have to consider your risk profile and time horizon when making investment decisions. Every portfolio has a liability or need to meet. Every investor has to understand their willingness, ability and need to take risk. And you still have to make sure you're invested in a way that suits not only your goals, but also your personality, time constraints and understanding of the markets.

David Swensen says that there are two types of investors and it's immensely important that institutions understand where they fit here:

Two types of investors inhabit the investment world - a vanishingly small group that makes high quality active management decisions and a much larger group that commands neither the resources nor the training to produce market-beating results. Membership in the active management cohort requires full-time dedication to understanding and exploiting market opportunities. Few qualify. Unfortunately, too many imagine that they possess active management skills, leading them to pursue costly strategies that all too predictably fail.

While the specific strategies will certainly differ depending on the individual or organization, the philosophy doesn't have to change. I'm often asked to explain the biggest differences between the institutional and individual investor. Here are the main points to consider:

Group Decisions. Institutions typically make decisions-by-committee which could include not only board members, but also a separate investment committee, as well as a fully staffed investment office or an outsourced consultant.

Size. Because institutions typically have much larger funds than individuals, they can gain access to different types of investments or money managers.

Time Horizons. Many endowments and foundations are set up to last in perpetuity, meaning more or less forever (or until the money runs out). Pension plans act as something of a large retirement account because they have stated liabilities to meet.

Taxes. Nonprofit institutions pay little-to-no taxes; a huge advantage when transacting in the marketplace, where taxes can take a huge chunk out of fund returns.

These differences are all seen as benefits to the institutional investor, but can turn into problems when not used correctly. Group decisions can become a burden if everyone is not on the same page. It can be difficult to accomplish your goals when you have competing egos, personalities and ideas.

While size can lead to lower fees, many institutions still choose to pay top dollar for the most expensive money managers. High fees are guaranteed; you don't always get what you pay for from investment products in terms of performance. Large investors are also constantly worried about impressing outsiders with their portfolios, when they should be focused internally on their own goals.

A long time horizon is perhaps the biggest benefit institutions have over the competition in the markets; yet, many squander it by focusing far too much on short-term performance and quarterly peer performance rankings. Career risk is another potential problem that causes many institutions to make short-term decisions with long-term capital at stake.

Removing the burden of taxes helps, but some institutions abuse this power, instead choosing to utilize hyperactive portfolio strategies that inflict unnecessary and avoidable costs or risks.

Many investors and trustees assume that the most important aspect of portfolio management is simply choosing the best investment opportunities at the right time. There's so much more that goes into running a successful investment program. I contend that the most important aspect of a successful institutional investment program starts with a successful organization and well-defined organizational culture. It's not investment alpha that matters, but organizational alpha.

Amazon founder and CEO Jeff Bezos once said, "We are stubborn on the vision. We are flexible on the details." My goal here is to provide institutional investors, trustees, board members and the beneficiaries of these funds the vision. From there, it's up to each fund to fill in the details, depending on their unique situation.

1. GOALS-BASED INVESTING

Here are five questions to consider as you read this chapter:

1. Why are we investing in the first place?
2. How can we align our investment plan with our stated mission?
3. How will we measure the success of our investment plan?
4. What is our organizational risk profile and time horizon?
5. How will we benchmark to our specific goals and needs to ensure we're on the right track?

If you went a doctor's office and they simply handed out medicine without first taking time to diagnose your ailment, you would think they were a terrible doctor. Yet this is exactly the way many in the financial industry operate. They prescribe solutions before they diagnose the underlying problems. They first create a product or portfolio and then try to convince people or organizations to invest in it. They try to make a sale without first gaining an understanding of their potential client's circumstances. It's completely backwards because you can't create an investment plan without a thorough understanding of a client's goals, needs, fears and expectations.

A number of years ago, the investment office I worked for took a meeting with a large, well-known consultant as a favor. We never planned on using this company's full consulting services, but thought it couldn't hurt to take the meeting to see how they viewed the world. The firm didn't really understand this dynamic and came into the meeting with guns blazing. They had a huge team with a well-rehearsed pitch they used to try to impress us. The head of the firm wasted no time going into his presentation along with some name-dropping of their current client base. He immediately outlined his firm's current investment views, which went something like this:

First of all, you need to have at least 15 percent of your portfolio invested in timber. And if you're not overweight in middle market mezzanine private equity funds and underweight large market LBOs you're going to be out of luck over the next decade. Who are your hedge fund managers? We have access to the best long/short manager in the business right now. How long will it take you to shift your portfolio to our platform?

We were immediately taken aback by the presumptuous nature of this pitch. Not only was this firm exceedingly overconfident in their outlook and abilities, but they never once asked us a single question about our organization before diving into their song and dance.

They didn't ask about the mission of our organization. They never asked what type of liquidity constraints we were under. They failed to try to gain a true sense of our risk profile and time horizon. They never asked what our stated return goals and assumptions were. They made no reference to our stated investment philosophy.

Needless to say, the meeting didn't last long. Maybe their performance would have been alright, but that's not the right way to approach portfolio management and investment planning because it will never work over the long-term. If you're not approaching the investment process from a goals-based perspective, it's going to be very difficult to ensure long-term success in the markets because even the best investment strategy in the world won't make a difference if the organization in question either can't or won't follow it through thick and thin.

Obviously, not every financial firm can individually vet every single client or prospect who is interested in their products or services. But when you're talking about institutional-level advisors or consultants who are providing a service to their clients, then they absolutely have to focus the majority of their time and energy on the client's needs. Financial services should not be a commodity business. It has to be personal for both parties to succeed. Certainly they can standardize the process, but they should always personalize the advice.

The problem is that many clients want to be wined and dined. They want someone to tell them exactly what they want to hear, even if it's an impossible strategy with unrealistic underlying assumptions. Wall Street is not the lone culprit in this game. After all, the consultant in my story had a very large book of business. They worked with a number of multi-billion dollar funds. Someone was eating up what they were putting out there. Charlie Munger once told a story that sums this up nicely:

> *I know one guy, he's extremely smart and a very capable investor. I asked him, 'What returns do you tell your institutional clients you will earn for them?' He said, '20%.' I couldn't believe it, because he knows that's impossible. But he said, 'Charlie, if I gave them a lower number, they wouldn't give me any money to invest!' The investment-management business is insane.*

Falling prey to this type of overconfidence and hubris is much harder to avoid when you don't have your investments aligned with your overall mission and goals. Here are a few more things I've learned over the years when it comes to goals-based investing:

Know what you own and why you own it. An investment firm can have the perfect sales pitch, investment structure, fund or opportunity. In many cases it may not matter if it doesn't fit within the client's stated investment policy. Just because there's a potential for a good investment opportunity doesn't mean it's the right fit for your portfolio. The markets are always tempting us with new products, risks and opportunities. This is how individuals and organizations end up investing in strategies they don't understand or have no business performing due diligence on in the first place. You have to know when to say no right away to save yourself the time and energy when something is obviously the wrong fit.

Personalize Your Benchmark. One of the reasons certain investors constantly change up their investment strategy - usually at the worst possible moment - is because they don't have the right benchmarks in place to begin with. Many don't even know how to define whether they're on track or not. And the number one benchmark for every investor should always be their personal goals; not peer performance, not the S&P 500, and not the latest fad investment. Your true risk as an organization is that you won't achieve either your short-term or long-term goals. Without a deep understanding of your goals from the start there's no way to judge your investments going forward. After all, achieving your goals is the whole point of investing in the first place.

Planning is a Process. It's perfectly acceptable to admit that your goals can and will change over time. We're all dealing with an uncertain future. No one knows how life is going to turn out. This is why the process of planning is so important. It allows you to continually work through the new challenges that may arise in the context of your stated plan. It's much easier to believe in certainty than process, but the right process can lead to much better outcomes in the end. This is why successful investment programs focus on process over outcomes when making high-quality decisions.

As we discussed earlier, institutional investors have some of the longest time horizons of any investor. But the boards of these funds are constantly worried about performance over the last month, quarter, or even year. It makes no sense. There is far too much emphasis on the short-term - geopolitical events, market timing, and tactical trading - and not nearly enough emphasis on the long-term - policy decisions, asset allocation, structural investment framework, process, and plan. However, it's those long-term decisions that will always trump short-term concerns.

Financial writer Morgan Housel has a great anecdote that illustrates this backwards line of thinking:

> *BlackRock CEO Larry Fink once told a story about having dinner with the manager of one of the world's largest sovereign wealth funds. The fund's objectives, the manager said, were generational.*
>
> *"So how do you measure performance?" Fink asked.*
>
> *"Quarterly," said the manager.*

This idea of making short-term decisions with long-term capital is one of the greatest sins of institutional asset management. The bulk of investment committee meetings and performance reviews are wasted obsessing over the latest crisis du jour or temporary market volatility, both of which usually end up being meaningless in the long-run. Unfortunately, the pull of peer performance reviews, noise from the financial media and our innate cognitive biases make it extraordinarily difficult to focus on the variables that truly matter.

Here's what happens when you make short-term decisions with long-term capital:

- You constantly change your strategy and chase past performance.
- You ignore any semblance of a long-term plan.
- You end up being reactive, instead of proactive, with your investment decisions.
- You incur higher fees from increased trading, due diligence and switching costs.
- You lose sight of your actual goals and time horizon.
- You end up with a portfolio that's built to withstand the last war, not win the next one.
- You lose out on most of the long-term benefits that come from diversification, rebalancing and mean reversion.

One of the best ways to combat the folly of short-run thinking is to ensure everyone on the team has a clearly defined role within the management of the fund in question. The fiduciary duty is by far the most important role to define so we tackle that in the next chapter.

2. DEFINING YOUR ROLE AS A FIDUCIARY

Here are five questions to consider as you read this chapter:

1. Do we understand our role as an acting fiduciary on behalf of this fund and its beneficiaries?
2. Do we have a documented decision-making process in place?
3. Are we following a structured investment process?
4. Are we more focused on long-term process or short-term outcomes?
5. Are the correct command and control steps laid out to ensure all roles are correctly defined?

Andrew Casperson had it all. He grew up in a family that was wealthy and well-connected. He was educated at some of the finest educational institutions in the world, including Princeton and Harvard. He went on to work for a well-known Wall Street firm where he was paid millions of dollars a year for his services. He was intelligent, had the pedigree, the prestige and the best education money can buy.

At face value, this sounds like the kind of person you want managing your money. Unfortunately, taking even the best resume in the world at face value doesn't mean you can automatically trust someone to manage your investments. After taking in money from friends, family members and clients, it was discovered that Mr. Casperson had defrauded his investors out of $38 million in a Ponzi Scheme.

It seems the people who gave him money simply believed his story and assumed he would make them money. When he pleaded guilty at his hearing he explained it this way: "The fraud was simple: I told family members and friends that a private equity firm had given me an allocation in a practically riskless debt instrument, and I offered them the opportunity to invest with me. I said that the debt instrument carried an interest rate of 15 to 20 percent."

The first lesson here is that if an investing opportunity sounds too good to be true, it probably is. Anyone who says they can guarantee you a double-digit rate of return on your capital with no risk is either delusional or lying, or maybe a combination of both.

One of Casperson's acquaintances told The Wall Street Journal, "Imagine if your brother or your best friend approached asking for a relatively small investment into something he did every day. This is a guy who had established himself as a respected and sophisticated investor for more than ten years at some of the most respected firms. Why wouldn't you put your money in?"

'Why wouldn't you put your money in?' is a great question. An even better one that investors should constantly be asking themselves is this: Why would you put your money in?

There is always an element of trust that occurs when you ask others to manage money on your behalf. But you can't blindly follow the advice of someone just because they have a prestigious background, attended elite colleges, or work for a big-name Wall Street firm. You can outsource money management, but you can never outsource your understanding about what's going on with your money. You still have to know what you're investing in and why. You have to monitor not only the potential rewards, but also the risks involved. You can't simply rubber stamp something because it sounds nice. A solid sales-pitch from a well-respected firm is not the same thing as independent oversight and advice.

My guess is none of Casperson's investors ever bothered to ask the following questions:

Where is the money being held and who has access to it?

Who can move the money and make trades?

What is the strategy and what are the risks involved?

How transparent is the process?

These are simple questions that every investor should be asking when turning their money over to someone else to manage it on their behalf. A true fiduciary would never have gotten caught up in a Ponzi Scheme such as this, but it happens all the time.

FIDUCIARY DUTY

In the introduction I described some of the main differences between individual and institutional investors - namely, the group dynamic in the decision-making process, the lack of tax constraints, larger funds to deal with, and differences in time horizons, goals and risk profiles. But I left one thing out, and it's a pretty big one, when you're describing nonprofits and charitable organizations - fiduciary duty.

Board members, and the investment committee specifically, are acting as trustees for the organization's assets on behalf of its beneficiaries. To the best of their ability, they must ensure that the finances are sound and fulfill their fiduciary duty. A fiduciary has legal and ethical responsibilities as a trustee to act in the best interests of their beneficiaries. Fiduciaries are those individuals who are tasked with overseeing the money or other assets of a person or organization.

Fiduciary duty requires board members to keep their personal feelings out of the equation. Fiduciaries should always act, first and foremost, for the good of the organization. This requires avoiding any conflicts of interest and being open, honest and transparent about the decisions being made on behalf of the organization. Fiduciaries should never put the organization at unavoidable or unnecessary risk. They need to ask the right questions and thoughtfully consider the right course of action. They need to understand where they do, and do not, add value. Board members can't be expected to be experts on all investment-related subject matters, but they should have a sound decision-making process in place to hire the right people for the job, when it makes sense to outsource certain capabilities.

There are three main responsibilities that you need to be aware of as a fiduciary:

1. Duty of Care. Duty of care requires that board members stay informed, regularly attend meetings, stay educated, provide guidance and use diligence and care when making decisions. They must oversee prudent use of all money, assets and people to ensure the organization's mission is being met. Fiduciaries should exercise independent judgment while making sound, informed decisions to ensure the organization is planning properly for the future. The board may not always be correct in the choices it makes, but they do have to be held accountable for their decision-making process.

2. Duty of Loyalty. Duty of loyalty requires that board members put the interests of the organization ahead of their own personal interests. The organization, or its assets, should not be used for personal gain. This means avoiding any conflicts of interest, such as self-dealing where you stand to gain financially from a nonprofit use of funds.

3. Duty of Obedience. Duty of obedience requires that board members comply with fiduciary law, act ethically and ensure that all federal, state and local laws are being followed. Activities and decisions should be done in accordance with the organization's stated mission. This means following stated guidelines, acting within the legal documents and creating policies to ensure all outside laws, rules and regulations are being followed as intended.

The correct governance structure needs to be in place to account for the resources, proficiency and board make-up of the fund in question. A strong investment committee brings discipline to the investment management process by vetting recommendations to ensure they fit within the stated mandate of the organization. Trustees should provide feedback, oversight, stay educated, improve the quality of decisions, perform sound judgment and understand where their strengths and weaknesses lie. They must maintain oversight on the organization's finances and stay accountable to donors and beneficiaries.

GOVERNING AND MANAGING FIDUCIARIES

There are two different ways to look at the management of financial assets in terms of the fiduciary duty:

1. Governing Fiduciary
2. Managing Fiduciary

The primary role of a governing fiduciary - the board members and investment committee - is managing the investment process, not managing the portfolio or making specific investment recommendations. In general, a fiduciary is not held liable for the overall investment performance of the fund. Instead, they are liable for the decision-making process. You can't always control the outcomes in the financial markets, but you do have control over the investment process used. Fiduciaries are judged according to whether the investment process fits the guidelines established by the organization and follows their specific investment plan.

On the other hand, a managing fiduciary could be a chief investment officer (CIO), consultant or advisor who is tasked with making specific investment recommendations for the organization to follow. The governing fiduciary is looking at things from 10,000 feet, while a managing fiduciary has boots on the ground by making sure things are functioning within the portfolio on a day-to-day basis. Most organizations don't have the resources to manage a portfolio and all that comes with it, so they often outsource the portfolio management function to a firm or firms that specialize in this field (more on this in Chapter 5). Managing fiduciaries are hired on behalf of the organization to provide guidance and advice and carry out those tasks in the investment process where they can help manage the portfolio more efficiently. It's up to the governing fiduciaries to ensure the managing fiduciaries are doing their job.

Governing and managing fiduciaries each have an obligation to aid each other in managing the overall investment management process by:

- Establishing investment guidelines and policies.
- Selecting asset classes and investment funds.
- Managing risk and monitoring performance results.
- Setting reasonable expectations to aid in future organizational decisions.

To fulfill their fiduciary duties, a fiduciary should:

- Implement well-informed policies for a thoughtful decision-making process.
- Prepare written documents that detail the investment process, including an Investment Policy Statement (IPS), Investment Committee Charter and Spending Policy Statement.
- Create a portfolio that is diversified according to the specific risk profile, time horizon and return objectives of the organization's mission and its beneficiaries.
- Avoid conflicts of interest and report any potential conflicts ahead of time.
- Control and account for all investment-related expenses and fees.

Breaches of fiduciary conduct include:

- Failing to follow a structured investment process.
- Failing to adhere to investment guidelines in the plan or trust documents.
- Failing to diversify the portfolio or selecting inappropriate asset classes.
- Failing to avoid prohibited transactions.

Managing the investment process and fulfilling your fiduciary duty can be accomplished by implementing a well thought-out decision-making process, which is the topic of the next chapter.

3. THE DECISION MAKING PROCESS

Here are five questions to consider as you read this chapter:

1. Are we following an evidence-based decision-making process?
2. What kind of investor are we and what is our edge?
3. Where are we making things too complex and how do we simplify our process?
4. How do we improve the continuity of our investment program?
5. How do we make everyone aware of their own inherent blind spots?

In the latest edition of David Swensen's previously mentioned book *Pioneering Portfolio Management*, there is a foreword written by legendary investment author and consultant, Charley Ellis. Ellis has witnessed Swensen's performance first hand for a number of years; initially, as a member of the Yale endowment investment committee, and, more recently, as chair of the endowment board. Ellis used his foreword to lay out six reasons for Swensen's success and enviable track record, which now spans a multi-decade period.

His reasons provide useful insights into what it takes to create not only a successful investment office, but a successful organizational culture in general. Here they are with a mixture of quotes from Ellis, and some paraphrasing on my part:

1. An Evidence-Based Decision-Making Process. Ellis says that Swensen uses, "A carefully constructed, rigorously tested portfolio structure and decision-making process that are clearly defensive." This one should be a no-brainer, but I'm always amazed at the amount of "trust me" or gut instinct decisions that pass for a legitimate process in the investment world.

2. A Team Effort. Swensen gets all the credit, but Ellis makes the point that it wouldn't be possible without a strong team behind him: "[T]he rich culture of professional respect and personal affection that bonds so many talented and committed individuals into a superbly effective team whose collective efforts excel." Swensen gets the most out of his team by trusting them and ignoring the standard office politics that ruin so many organizations from within. This is also important for the continuity of the fund going forward.

3. Professional Respect. The respect and trust extends beyond the team members of Yale's investment office to their third-party, outside money managers. It's a give and take relationship as Swensen always looks to help others who are more than willing to reciprocate. People are actively looking for ways to help him and his team.

4. A Focus on the Client. Ellis says that, "Swensen & co. are extraordinarily thoughtful about their engagement with their client, Yale University." In addition to the typical portfolio management responsibilities that come with running a large endowment fund, Swensen devotes much of his time thinking about the best interests of the institution; including their long-term goals and spending needs. Focusing on your client's needs should always be job number one, but it's something that is often overlooked in the mainly sales-first, client-second mindset of the financial industry.

5. Personal Respect and Affection. Ellis claims this may be the most important secret to Yale's success: "Visitors to Yale's Investment Office are invariably impressed by the open architecture and informal 'happy ship' climate that is almost as obvious as the disciplined intensity with which the staff work at their tasks and responsibilities." The outcome of creating an inviting organizational culture is happier employees, which means very low turnover in staff. I'm always amazed when companies don't go out of their way to create a workplace where people actually want to work.

6. Integrity. "There's more money than certified talent in the world of investing, so outstanding investment managers have many choices because so many investors want to be their clients. Given their freedom of choice, managers prefer to work for and with clients they like and admire, and they like and admire David Swensen very much," says Ellis. This one may seem obvious - of course money managers want to work Swensen and Yale - but Ellis makes the Darwinian point that social desirability trumps competitive strength in this case.

Few investment organizations in the world could ever come close to matching Yale's investment performance over the long-run. And those who try are usually looking in the wrong place. They want to know how to pick the best money managers, like Yale does; how to structure their portfolio, just like Swensen; or how to match his returns.

These copycats have it all backwards. They want all the answers but they're not even asking the right questions. They're all looking for the tactics to employ without first ensuring they have the correct organizational structure in place. There's no way that Swensen would have enjoyed his level of success without creating the right atmosphere from the start. He has the support of his University. He has an investment committee that trusts his judgment and allows him to do his job without the shackles of short-term performance concerns.

Although it may seem odd to some that Ellis described so many non-investment-related reasons to define Swensen's success over the years, it's those intangibles that have made the biggest difference. I also find it telling that Ellis is one of the foremost proponents for simple investment strategies for nearly everyone else, outside of Yale. He knows what it takes to produce the level of performance Swensen has put up over the years and understands that it's not something that can be easily replicated.

WINNING THE LOSER'S GAME

In his own classic investment book, *Winning the Loser's Game*, Ellis describes three different ways to succeed and make money in the markets. Each one is exhausting in its own way:

1. Option Number One is Physically Exhausting. You work harder than the competition. You try to do more in hopes of gaining an informational edge.

2. Option Number Two is Mentally Exhausting. You're more intelligent than the competition. This one can only be used by a handful of investors. The usual suspects that come to mind have names like Buffett, Munger, Soros, Klarman, Druckenmiller and even Swensen. These people were born to do this and should come with a "do not try this at home" disclaimer.

3. Option Number Three is Emotionally Exhausting. You try to remain more rational than the competition and utilize a long-term process. You must have a long-term approach with a very patient, disciplined strategy that can be difficult to follow in the short-term. You can never get too hot or too cold and have to remain rational, even when those around you are acting irrational.

The only way any of these methods work in the end is if other investors are wrong about which group they're really meant for. Many professional investors assume that they fall into group two, while an even larger group tries their hand in group one to make up for any shortfall in intelligence. There are always going to be people who are smarter than you in the markets and working harder doesn't necessarily lead to better results. Therefore, the third option offers the best chance for the majority of investors to succeed.

But an emotionally exhausting investment approach offers its own set of challenges. You have to focus on a long-term process and learn to ignore short-term outcomes. It could take anywhere from five to twenty years to see the best results. Shorter time frames in the one- to four-year range won't always lead to favorable outcomes. You have to be willing to accept volatility and abandon the quest for short-term alpha. It's also boring and not as exciting to take a longer-term stance in the markets. And maybe the hardest part of all is that it's much easier to do something rather than nothing, even when doing nothing is the right move most of the time. The truly sophisticated investor knows exactly where they fall on this spectrum and doesn't try to do more than they are capable of doing. This is easier said than done.

SIMPLICITY

Tren Griffin tells a great joke in his book, *Charlie Munger: The Complete Investor*, that describes the needless complexity many intelligent people try to inject into the decision-making process:

> *Too many people take a situation and create complexity where none is needed. Take, for example, the old joke about unnecessary complexity at the National Aeronautics and Space Administration (NASA). The storyteller starts by saying that early in the space program NASA discovered that ballpoint pens would not work in zero gravity. NASA scientists spent a decade and huge amounts of money developing a pen that wrote not only in zero gravity but on almost any surface, at extremely low temperatures, and in any position of the astronaut. The punch line is: the Russians instead used a pencil.*

The first thing that popped into my mind when reading this was that far too many institutional investors act like NASA in this situation. They take the complicated route to try to solve a problem without even considering the simple one that's staring them right in the face. Nearly every great investor, intellectual or business person I've read about over the years discusses the importance of simplifying in order to succeed. Here is a sampling:

> *"Simple can be harder than complex: You have to work hard to get your thinking clean to make it simple. But it's worth it in the end because once you get there, you can move mountains." - Steve Jobs*

"The business schools reward difficult complex behavior more than simple behavior, but simple behavior is more effective." - *Warren Buffett*

"The five ascending levels of intelligence: smart, intelligent, brilliant, genius, simple." - *Albert Einstein*

"It is remarkable how much long-term advantage people like us have gotten by trying to be consistently not stupid, instead of trying to be very intelligent." - *Charlie Munger*

Yet, the majority of institutional investors are constantly looking for ways to make things more complicated. Why is this the case? Here are four reasons:

1. It's Interesting. What sounds more stimulating as an allocator of capital? Traveling to New York, Silicon Valley and London for due diligence trips to meet with hedge fund, private equity and venture capital managers; getting wined and dined with free food and booze while getting to hear about complicated strategies, alpha, new technologies and 'what sets us apart' in an effort to beat the market and your peers. Or choosing a sensible asset allocation, keeping costs low, staying operationally efficient, avoiding crippling mistakes, setting reasonable goals and doing nothing most the of time.

It's obvious why the majority of large investors choose option a, but that doesn't mean these funds will be better off financially from this decision.

2. They Think It's Their Job to Outperform. Most institutional investors assume their job is to outperform the markets and their benchmarks to earn their keep (and most likely a performance bonus). Most board members are also very successful in business, ultra-competitive and want nothing more than to beat the performance numbers from endowments like Harvard and Yale. But it's not enough to beat their peers. Many also have to somehow prove their intellectual superiority by making their portfolios and strategies so opaque that most people within the organization have no idea how the money is actually being managed. It's an ego contest. Everyone wants to beat everyone else even with different goals and somehow complexity becomes the norm.

3. They Assume Complex Must be Better. The investors that run complex portfolios are highly educated individuals who are very intelligent. It can be hard for them to admit that a simpler solution makes the most sense. There is a false sense of security in doing what everyone else is doing.

The assumption is that complex financial markets require complex solutions, but new and exciting is not the same thing as useful.

4. Social Validation. Psychologist Robert Cialdini has shown that one of the main filters we use to make decisions is by looking at the decisions of others. Social proof is the idea that it feels more comfortable to go along with the crowd when making tough decisions on our own because we look at what others are doing in times of uncertainty. Investors with lots of money at stake tend to feel that they have to use "sophisticated" investment strategies that cost a lot of money in order to keep up with their peers. I've seen complexity fail over multiple investment cycles in these types of portfolios, but as Keynes told us, "Worldly wisdom teaches that it is better for the reputation to fail conventionally than to succeed unconventionally." Simplicity has become the exception, while complexity is now the rule.

CONTINUITY

The average tenure for a chief investment officer of a state-run pension fund is just five years. The average tenure for a board member is also five years. Then there's the revolving door of different consultants and money managers that institutions go through on a regular basis. All of which leads to continuous changes in funds, money managers, asset classes and investment styles.

Running a complex, unique style of portfolio management might impress the boosters, but it's terrible from a continuity standpoint. You give yourself the potential to hit a homerun, but at the risk of striking out. It's also remarkably difficult to keep a unique portfolio structure in place if the person or persons who put it together leave(s) the organization. One of the biggest benefits of a simpler approach is the fact that it offers an organization more continuity in their investment program over time. Of course, this requires more planning up front in terms of goal-setting, expectation-setting and defining your investment philosophy (more on this in Chapter 4).

Complex portfolio structures are an operationally inefficient way to invest and requires serious time, effort and resources to pull it off. Very few organizations can thread the needle in this way. And, even if you have all of those things in place, there's no guarantee of success. Increasing the number of fund types you implement only increases the operational risk, due diligence costs and monitoring problems.

All that aside, it becomes nearly impossible to implement a consistent investment plan over time when you increase the complexity of your portfolio. Multi-billion dollar funds can afford the luxury of experimenting with how they run their investment offices. They have huge donor bases that refill their coffers every year. For everyone else, however, the simpler and more consistent the approach, the better.

WHY WE MAKE POOR DECISIONS

Take a look at the following set of lines and try to match up the first one all the way to the left with the three choices on the right:

A cursory glance at line A shows that it's too short while line B looks far too tall, so the obvious answer is line C, which looks to be the exact same height as our line on the left. Simple enough. But when Solomon Asch performed this experiment with groups of people he found some startling revelations about peer pressure and our willingness to conform with others, even when presented with compelling evidence to the contrary.

Asch put together a group of eight people, yet seven were actually people that he placed into the study with specific instructions about what to do. The seven "plants" in the study were told to give varying answers in the eighteen different tests they were to run, but they were all to give the same answer at the same time. So sometimes they picked the correct line (C) while other times they all agreed on the incorrect choice (A or B). Asch ran over one hundred trials and found that nearly 40 percent of the time the independent subject conformed with the group's wrong answer. Instead of using their own common sense, they went along with the herd because it felt more comfortable. Asch called this social conformity, where social influence can lead to a change in belief or action to fit in during a group setting.

Making decisions as an individual can be difficult, as you can see from the long list of behavioral biases in Table 3.1, due to our innate human nature. But when you add in a group dynamic, these forces can all combine together into what Charlie Munger calls the lollapalooza effect. For example, the Great Financial Crisis of 2007-2009 was something of lollapalooza event. Many different factors came together as problems multiplied over a number of decades and finally came to a head, leading to the worst economic crisis since the Great Depression.

Table 3.1

Loss Aversion: Losing hurts twice as bad as gains feel good.
Confirmation Bias: Seeking opinions or data that agree with prior beliefs.
Anchoring: Analyzing from a default starting point that can influence conclusions.
Endowment Bias: Placing a higher value on something currently possessed.
Hindsight Bias: Assuming the past was easier to foresee than it actually was.
Dunning-Kruger Effect: We have a hard time seeing our own ignorance.
Sunk Cost Fallacy: Decisions are determined by investments already made.
Cognitive Dissonance: It's uncomfortable to holding two competing beliefs at once.
Disposition Effect: Holding money losers too long while sell money winners too fast.
Framing: How choices are presented can affect our conclusions.
Illusion of Control: Believing we have control over uncontrollable outcomes.
Availability Heuristic: Recalling something easily increases its importance.
Representativeness: Classifying new information based on past experiences.
Status Quo: Sticking with what we've always done instead of changing course.
Self-Attribution: Taking credit for wins but blaming others for losses.
Gambler's Fallacy: Seeing patterns where none exist in sequences of random events.

The lollapalooza effect is what happens when multiple forces combine to produce either wonderful or terrible results, depending on how well they mesh together. Dealing with large groups of people means that there will always be trade-offs, leaving many unhappy all at once if things aren't managed correctly. This can lead to negative lollapalooza effects.

For example, a study of U.S. federal judges found that judges working alone took a relatively extreme course of action only 30 percent of the time. When they were working in groups of three, this figure more than doubled, to 65 percent. It's much easier for things to get out of control in a group setting. This is why individuals often do things during a protest they would never do if when acting out on their own. The herd mentality is a powerful driving force behind our actions.

The goal should be to harness the positive benefits of the lollapalooza effect. As with almost everything, there are pros and cons to the group dynamic. On the positive side, you can end up with a diversity of opinions and people who can play Devil's Advocate to look at a problem from every angle. On the negative side, you can end up with a herd mentality or similar group of like-minded people who simply multiply the confirmation bias as a whole.

The point here is not to show that we're all predisposed to make poor decisions. The point is to get people and organizations to recognize we all have blind spots. Our emotions aren't always going to take us down the wrong path, but we do have to admit that they exist and shape our views in many ways that we may not be aware of.

HOW TO MAKE BETTER DECISIONS

So how do you make better decisions in the face of uncertainty? What follows are six ways to improve upon your decision-making process.

1. Perform a Pre-Mortem. The only certainty about financial markets is the fact that you are bound to be surprised by what happens. The trick is to make sure you're never surprised that you're surprised. Uncertainty needs to be built into the decision-making process. Things will go wrong. Tough decisions will have to be made at times. Consider what would happen if your decisions led to a huge success. Now consider what would happen if your decisions led to an enormous failure. Figure out a way to meld the two together to see how the potential successes and failures could be used to make better decisions. It's easy to look for ways to be successful, but the best decision-makers understand how to deal with potential problems areas. When you envision what could go wrong in advance, and build in contingencies for those episodes, you lower the chances that you'll panic at the wrong time and make a huge mistake.

Because of hindsight bias, investors are constantly performing post-mortems. While it makes sense to learn from your mistakes, by positioning your portfolio entirely on what you wish you would have done in the past you will always be one step behind the markets; chasing past performance. Investing success comes from setting reasonable expectations ahead of time and anticipating the fact that occasionally things don't work out as planned.

2. Document and Utilize Checklists. Writing down the reasons for all of your decisions can lower the chances of hindsight bias creeping in and compounding potentially poor outcomes. The past will always look easy while the future will always seem messy and uncertain. Having documentation in place that lays out the 'what?' and the 'why?' of your decisions can help when looking back after the fact. (More on the documentation involved in the investment process in Chapter 7.)

3. Stay Humble. Markets are complex adaptive systems. This means any hope for certainty needs to be thrown out the window. No one can forecast what will happen with either the markets or the economy on a consistent basis. You're not only trying to predict what will happen, but also how other market participants will react when something happens. This is not a game to be taken lightly. Be humble in your approach or the market will humble you.

4. No Blame or Excuses. You're not always going to get the best outcomes but that's not the point of a good process. A good process is about making high-probability decisions. No one is good enough to be right all the time.

Philip Tetlock has spent his career studying forecasters, how accurate their predictions are (not very) and the typical excuses they make when they're wrong. Tetlock has studied experts in a wide variety of fields from politics to economics to investing and basically found that these experts were right at a rate that is lower than the flip of a coin. And, as their confidence in a prediction goes up, the results don't get any better than the forecasts they're not as sure about.

Throughout his research he came up with five excuses that experts make on a regular basis when they're wrong:

1. The "if only" clause: If only this one thing would have gone my way I would have been right.
2. The "ceteris paribus" clause: Something completely unexpected happened so it's not my fault.
3. The "it almost occurred" clause: It didn't happen but I was close.
4. The "just wait" clause: I'm not wrong, I'm just early.
5. The "don't hold it against me" clause: It's just one prediction.

Pay attention to see if your team, your money managers or your consultants are constantly coming up with these types of excuses. Moving the goalposts after the fact is a huge red flag. You have to own your decisions. You won't always like the outcomes, but trying to blame others for your decisions is a good way to ruin a useful process.

5. Scenario Analysis. Technology now makes it easier than ever to simulate a wide range of outcomes using both historical and expected risk and return data. There are programs you can purchase that cost tens of thousands of dollars or ones that you can use for free. It all depends on the amount of detail you would like to work with. As with all models, these Monte Carlo simulations are all garbage-in, garbage-out so you have to be realistic when using them. The biggest benefit of using scenario analysis software is that it allows you to test your current assumptions and risk-return expectations. It allows you to look at best and worst case scenarios and, more importantly, plan for a wide range of outcomes. These simulations will never help you predict the future, but they can help you prepare for it, which is all you can hope for in lieu of a functioning crystal ball. As the old saying goes, better to be vaguely right than precisely wrong.

6. Make it a Habit. Habits are beneficial because they allow the brain to ramp down from time to time, something it needs because the brain can get tired just like other any other part of your body.

In his book, *The Power of Habit: Why We Do What We Do in Life and*

Business, Charles Duhigg discusses the career of former Super Bowl champion NFL coach, Tony Dungy, and how he used the ordinary to beat the extraordinary. When he was an assistant coach early on in his career Dungy was constantly passed over for head coaching jobs. In part this had to do with his philosophy, which was far too simple for many organizations.

During interviews he would explain his belief that the key to winning was changing the habits of his players. He was more focused on process than gut instinct. Dungy wanted his players to simply react during games and stop making so many decisions. Dungy proclaimed, "Champions don't do extraordinary things. They do ordinary things, but they do them without thinking. They follow the habit they've learned."

When Dungy was finally hired by the Tampa Bay Buccaneers it only took him a few years to turn around what was once the laughing stock of the league. The players bought into his philosophy, but it seemed to breakdown in big games. When talking to his players after the losses it turned out they would forget their habits during critical plays and revert to their old instinct-based ways. Dungy eventually instilled in his players the idea that you have to believe in the system at all times, not just when you feel like it.

Dungy was fired by the Bucs after a few consecutive losses in the conference championship game, but eventually went on to win a Super Bowl with the Indianapolis Colts because the players finally trusted his process-based philosophy in big games. Dungy said he wasn't trying to completely change the players on his team. At that stage in their career it would make little sense to go for a complete overhaul. What he was trying to do was instill a process that would allow them to make better decisions with the talents they already possessed.

This is a worthy goal when trying to improve your investment process, as well. Investors assume they need to do extraordinary things in order to succeed, but they do so at the expense of the ordinary things which are so important, yet often overlooked. Having a solid process in place that allows you to make the right decisions without thinking about them is such an unbelievably huge advantage when dealing with the inherent uncertainty in financial markets. Duhigg says in the book that, "willpower becomes habit by choosing a certain behavior ahead of time, and then following that routine when an inflection point arrives." The inflection points in the markets are where the biggest mistakes are made by investors.

Making fewer decisions under stressful situations is a net positive. You can't pick and choose when to follow your system. As long as you make good decisions ahead of time you should rarely, if ever, override a good process.

This is why you never want to judge your success or failure exclusively based on short-term outcomes or anchor yourself to past forecasts. Sometimes the right decision leads to a poor outcome because luck plays such a large role in shaping the markets and the economy. One of the worst things that can happen to an organization is that they make a terrible decision but get bailed out because they were lucky. That's no way to build a sustainable investment program because luck eventually runs out. Poor outcomes that result within the framework of a good process will happen from time to time, but they shouldn't be confused with good outcomes that result from a poor process.

In the next chapter we'll talk about the importance of understanding who you are as an investor as it relates to the investment process.

4. THE INVESTMENT PROCESS

Here are five questions to consider as you read this chapter:

1. What is our overarching investment philosophy?
2. Can we explain our strategy in a way that everyone understands it?
3. When do we make portfolio changes and why?
4. Have we developed an organizational margin of safety if we're wrong?
5. What does our due diligence policy look like?

Shawshank Redemption is arguably one of the best, most re-watchable movies of all-time. The lead character in the movie, Andy Dufresne (played masterfully by Tim Robbins), is convicted of a crime he did not commit. It takes Dufresne 20 years to slowly dig his way out of his cell using a simple rock hammer and a series of posters to conceal the hole in his cell wall. Dufresne was a businessman and accountant who knew his way around finances, which ultimately set him up for when he escaped.

When thinking about creating a sustainable investment program, it can make sense to think about the big picture perspective from an Andy Dufresne perspective. My Shawshank rules are as follows:

If I unexpectedly went to jail for 10-20 years, how would I setup my investment process so that it could still more or less function without me at the helm?

How do I set up a decision-making process that would allow for high-quality decisions even when I'm not around anymore?

How do I ensure continuity in our investment program and philosophy if there are changes made to the leadership of this organization and investment committee?

Obviously, you can't simply set an investment program on autopilot and forget about it over time (although many funds would probably see an improvement in performance if they did this). Decisions will need to be made depending on how things turn out in the constantly evolving markets and the state of the organization or fund in question. The point of this exercise is to think long and hard about the big decisions up front; things like investment philosophy, policy guidelines, documentation and the decision-making process. One of the most important first steps is figuring out the type of investor you are, not necessarily who you would like to be.

DEFINING YOUR INVESTMENT PHILOSOPHY

There was a story told before Super Bowl XLIX, which pitted the New England Patriots against the Seattle Seahawks, about Seattle's coach, Pete Carroll, and his off-season speaking gigs at conferences. Carroll is a high-energy, high-enthusiasm coach, so he gives motivational speeches to corporate leaders, other coaches, investors and even members of the military in his down time. In his talks he begins with a simple task for the audience: "Raise your hand if you have a philosophy for your team or organization."

Of course, everyone in the room always raises their hand. What kind of leader would you be if you didn't have an overarching philosophy? Carroll then hits everyone who has their hand up with a follow-up question, by asking, "Can you describe your philosophy in 25 words or less?"

At this point, basically everyone's hand would go down.

Carroll has been known to ask this question when he interviews prospective assistant coaches for his staff, as well. It's not necessarily that the philosophy has to be perfect, but it's the process of actually thinking it through and developing it in the first place that makes a difference. Those who can effectively communicate their philosophy have a leg up on the competition.

Every investor should also be able to explain their investment philosophy. Maybe it doesn't have to be in 25 words or less, but if you're not able to explain your philosophy in a 60-second elevator pitch, chances are you haven't truly developed a viable process in the first place.

An investment philosophy is simply a set of principles that will guide your actions when making portfolio decisions at both the macro and micro levels. Philosophy should be the starting point for every other portfolio-related decision you make as an investor. With an abundance of research, data and opinions at our fingertips in today's fast-paced world it becomes easy to fall into the trap of always trying to locate the best money managers, strategies or securities to get into *right now*.

This is a patchwork system that is sure to fail. Without an overarching philosophy to bring it all together, you'll just be chasing one investment fad to the next, losing money along the way. It may seem like a minor distinction, but an investment philosophy must be determined before a portfolio strategy can be implemented. Philosophy is the vision while strategy is the details.

It's not a simple exercise, but I've prepared 10 questions everyone should ask themselves when considering an investment philosophy:

1. What are your core investment beliefs?
2. Do you understand your philosophy and why you believe in it?
3. Do you know the potential risks?
4. Does it suit your personality and individual circumstances?
5. Will your philosophy help you follow the strategy you choose?
6. What constraints are necessary for turning your philosophy into a portfolio?
7. What will you own and why will you own it?
8. What will cause you to buy or sell?
9. What will cause you to make changes to your portfolio over time?
10. What types of investments or strategies will you avoid?

SHRINKING ALPHA

One of the biggest factors that investors have to deal when turning their philosophy into a strategy is trying to figure out where their opportunity set lies. Competition in the markets has never been stronger, making it harder than ever to earn the elusive market outperformance that so many institutional investors actively seek.

In their book, *The Incredible Shrinking Alpha*, authors and investors Larry Swedroe and Andrew Berkin lay out the case - backed up with loads of academic research - that risk-adjusted outperformance, or alpha in industry-speak, is becoming harder than ever to come by these days. But the reason has nothing to do with the old theory that a dart-throwing monkey can beat the investment professionals because they're all really emperors with no clothes. In fact, it's the opposite. Professional investors are more informed, more highly educated and more competitive than ever before. Yet they are all competing for a shrinking slice of the alpha pie.

This is what author Michael Mauboussin calls the paradox of skill. Mauboussin says, "It's not that managers have gotten dumber. It's precisely the opposite. The average manager is more skillful than in past years. The paradox of skill says that when the outcome of an activity combines skill and luck, as skill improves, luck becomes more important in shaping results." How many institutional investors bother to ask themselves if the investment managers they are investing with are lucky or truly exhibit skill?

Swedroe and Berkin go on to cite the work of David Hsieh, a finance professor at Duke University's business school, who concluded that there is roughly $30 billion of available alpha for the entire hedge fund industry. It's impossible to know if this number is correct or not, but let's assume it is for the sake of argument. In 1990, there were roughly 600 hedge funds managing close to $40 billion in assets. Today there are well over 10,000 hedge funds collectively managing close to $3 trillion. That $30 billion in alpha is much easier to share when there are fewer funds. The opportunities that were once available to these funds just aren't quite there anymore.

Author and investor William Bernstein performed a study on hedge funds for his book *Skating Where the Puck Was*, where he looked at the returns on a large series of hedge fund returns and ran a regression against a three-factor model to determine the source of the performance for these funds. In the initial 1998 to 2002 period, hedge funds actually earned their keep, producing alpha of 9 percent. Unfortunately, it didn't last long as investors showered these funds with capital following the severe bear market of 2000-2002. This performance chase shrunk the alpha earned by this group in the 2003-2007 period to -0.7 percent. Then from 2008-2012 alpha went negative to -4.5 percent. The increased competition and larger capital base made it nearly impossible for these funds to keep up their outperformance.

It's likely never been harder to outperform as an institutional investor and the numbers back this up. Standard & Poor's puts out a regular report that measures the number of mutual funds that beat their benchmarks and the numbers are always fairly low, making it a low probability bet to outperform a simple index. But surely institutional investors have an easier time, considering they can gain scale through their higher asset bases by investing in separately-managed accounts with lower fees, right?

Percentage of Domestic Equity Managers Underperforming Over Five Years			
Category	Benchmark	Mutual Funds (%)	Institutional Accounts
All Domestic	S&P Composite 1500	88.43	85.00
All Large Cap	S&P 500	84.15	85.81
All Mid Cap	S&P Mid Cap 400	76.69	64.71
All Small Cap	S&P Small Cap 600	90.13	81.82
All Multi Cap	S&P Composite 1500	88.56	83.20
Large Cap Growth	S&P 500 Growth	86.54	89.89
Large Cap Core	S&P 500	88.26	86.54
Large Cap Value	S&P 500 Value	82.17	73.79
Mid Cap Growth	S&P Mid Cap 400 Growth	81.48	68.00
Mid Cap Core	S&P Mid Cap 400	76.51	64.29
Mid Cap Value	S&P Mid Cap 400 Value	70.27	58.33
Small Cap Growth	S&P Small Cap 600 Growth	91.89	87.10
Small Cap Core	S&P Small Cap 600	91.44	81.48
Small Cap Value	S&P Small Cap 600 Value	92.31	76.67
Multi Cap Growth	S&P Composite 1500 Growth	90.57	81.25
Multi Cap Core	S&P Composite 1500	91.16	84.09
Multi Cap Value	S&P Composite 1500 Value	76.67	79.59
Emerging Markets	S&P Emerging BMI	69.94	49.51
Global	S&P Global 1200	78.97	62.04
International	S&P 700	55.37	29.05
International Small Cap	S&P Ex-U.S. Small Cap	47.37	19.61
Real Estate	S&P United States REIT	82.64	27.27

Source: S&P Dow Jones Indices LLC, eVestment Alliance, CRSP. Data as of Dec. 31, 2015

Not so, as you can see from the data in the previous table. S&P looked at both mutual funds and institutional separately managed accounts to see how many funds in a wide variety of asset classes outperform their benchmarks over a 5-year stretch. Institutional money managers find it just as difficult to beat their benchmarks as mutual funds do in the majority of fund categories. A large percentage of institutional money managers don't beat their benchmarks, meaning it's a low probability event for institutions to pick the best performers over time.

THE HERD MENTALITY

So why do these large funds, armed with teams of consultants and professional money managers at their disposal, have such a hard time outperforming simple index funds and benchmarks?

Following the technology boom and bust and the Great Financial Crisis, many institutions decided to rethink the entire way they constructed their portfolios. In many cases that meant ditching the more conventional approach to money management of using stocks and bonds. So many of these funds were caught offside in these stock market crashes that many made the mistake of fighting the last war, something institutional investors seem to do on a regular basis. Take a look at the numbers in Table 4.2 which shows the results from a study performed for the *Journal of Finance* on the perils of chasing performance by institutional investors.

The "smart" money has a nasty habit of buying winning funds *after* they've just won and selling losing funds *after* they've just lost, allowing them to miss out on the mean reversion which often accompanies above or below average performance.

The following chart shows how institutional investment committees continually make their investment manager decisions based on past performance, only to be disappointed by the subsequent returns after making manager changes. They hired managers that had recently outperformed and fired managers that had recently underperformed only to see those roles reverse after their investment moves were made. The funds they fired went on to show better performance than the ones they hired in their place, a backwards buy high, sell low strategy.

Institutional Investment Management Hire/Fire Decisions: 1996-2003

Source: "The Selection and Termination of Investment Management Firms by Plan Sponsors," Amit Goyal, Sunil Wahal (The Journal of Finance, Volume 63, Issue 4, printed August 2008) Data: 8,775 hiring decisions by 3,417 plan sponsors delegating $627 billion in assets; 869 firing decisions by 482 plan sponsors withdrawing $105 billion in assets. Analysis covers the period 1996 through 2003.

Many institutions run a manager-of-managers approach where they try to continually pick the best active money managers to invest money on their behalf in the various asset classes and strategies. When running a manager-of-managers approach, not only do you have to pick the best active managers, you also have to fire them and find new ones. That leaves multiple chances to be wrong. And, because so many funds try to do this on a consistent basis as opposed to forming long-term partnerships with their investments, it opens them up to being wrong over and over again. The greater the number of decisions that are made, the lower the probability for success and the higher the probability for chasing past performance. If picking one successful manager that can outperform is difficult, how hard must it be to pick dozens and dozens (which many institutions try to do)?

There are plenty of great portfolio managers out there. But there probably aren't enough asset allocators or organizations who can discern the right time to invest with a great portfolio manager and when it's time to move on. This process is made even more difficult when a large committee has to come together to make group decisions.

It's not simply that markets are hard. There are many external factors that cause the performance chase to continue. When you manage large sums of money - like a pension, endowment, foundation or family office - there's no shortage of funds looking to pitch you. New investment opportunities are seemingly endless. The temptation is always there to make changes to your portfolio. There's always a new shiny object to draw your attention and every money manager makes a great sales pitch in trying to prove they're all special snowflakes.

Investment officers and consultants also have to justify the fees they're being paid. Doing nothing, even when it's the right thing to do, isn't easy when others expect to see positive short-term results at all times. The best thing you can do as a fiduciary is stand between your decision-makers and a huge mistake at the wrong time; easier said than done during a period of poor relative or absolute performance. Hiring and firing managers is also a nice way to find someone else to blame for poor performance. Career risk can be a deadly factor to even a solid investment plan.

Putting together a portfolio using a manager-of-managers approach is highly difficult. Not only is it tough to beat the market, but there is a ton of work involved when trying to perform due diligence, monitor and manage an entire group of money managers.

DUE DILIGENCE

Winning the loser's game means it's much easier to figure out the mistakes other investors make and try to avoid them, but at a certain point you actually have to have a process for selecting and judging investment opportunities. Here are some thoughts on the abilities necessary to perform high quality investment due diligence:

The ability to say no over and over again. The nonprofit investment office I used to work for had a fairly large endowment, but in the institutional space we were still considered something of a mid-sized fund in comparison to the much larger pension plans, Ivy League endowments and sovereign wealth funds out there. Even as a relatively small player we would still receive something on the order of 10 to 15 cold calls or emails a week from money managers and funds looking to pitch us. The number of available investment options seems almost unlimited when you include categories such as private equity, hedge funds, real estate and venture capital on top of the standard stock and bond fund managers.

Having a strict investment criterion is exceedingly important because there will always be the temptation to make changes by adding new funds to the mix. Many of these funds have some of the best sales and marketing teams in the finance industry so they all sound like amazing opportunities when they get you on the phone or in person for a meeting. The trick is having the ability to say no to good or even great investments when they aren't in your wheelhouse or when they aren't a great fit within your portfolio or risk profile. A good set of guidelines about what it is you won't invest in is just as important as outlining those characteristics that you will invest in.

The ability to judge the character of a portfolio manager and an organization's culture. In some ways you almost have to be better at judging people than judging investments to succeed in this endeavor.

Because you're dealing with such intelligent people on the investment side and such skilled salespeople on the marketing side, you have to have a really good BS detector to see through the sales pitch from fund firms and portfolio managers.

Every fund will talk about what "differentiates their firm" or process from the market and their competition. Every fund has a detailed pitch book of marketing materials and a highly educated staff. You can't get caught up in the narrative or become blinded by the brilliance of a slick portfolio manager. You have to avoid placing a charisma premium on money managers that are impressive in a meeting to be able to see through to the actual process behind the story.

The CIO of a large college endowment once told me his fund hired private investigators to run thorough background checks on every single portfolio manager and team they hired. While this may seem like the prudent thing to do, shouldn't it be a red flag if you don't trust someone enough that you have to bring in Magnum P.I. to sort through their trash can? And don't you think these people are already pretty good at hiding the skeletons in their closet if they've built billion-dollar investment firms?

If you're not able to judge the people behind the investment process to know that you're working with an honest, trustworthy firm, it probably won't matter how the investments perform. You have to be able to develop long-term working relationships with people and firms of high character. This extends beyond treating their clients with respect. They have to also be good to their employees. An arrogant, self-absorbed portfolio manager might be a great investor, but odds are eventually they'll come back to haunt you at some point. And if a fund manager makes it sound like they're doing you a favor by letting you invest in his or her fund, it's probably best to sit that one out. There are countless other options out there today.

The ability to know when a process is done working and when it's just out of style. One of the hardest decisions to make in the investment world is distinguishing between an investment style that's out of favor for the time being and one that doesn't really work anymore. There will always be doubt that creeps in when poor performance occurs. That's natural. But in this business you really have to own your decisions. You have to be able to understand why something works over the long-term, but not right now; and also why it should continue to work in the future. And you can never become married to an investment or manager when it's not working anymore.

No one can ever know for certain whether a manager, fund or strategy is done working or is simply out of style at the moment, but there is a good way to test your own fortitude and faith in an investment. If you see poor performance for two or three years, would you be more than happy to invest more money in that fund? If not, you probably don't trust it enough so why stay invested in the first place? If yes, you've made the decision to be a long-term, disciplined investor by rebalancing into weakness. Every investment will test your faith at one time or another. It's not always a bad thing to move on and cut ties, but there has to be a better reason other than 'performance hasn't been so great lately.' Performance should be thought of both quantitatively and qualitatively.

To state the obvious, none of these intangibles in the due diligence process are easy. But no one ever said successful investing was easy.

THERE'S NEVER BEEN A BETTER TIME TO BE AN INVESTOR

Following the success of *Pioneering Portfolio Management*, Swensen decided to write a book that was geared towards individual investors and those smaller and mid-sized institutions that don't have the bandwidth that Yale's investment office has to pull off the active management approach they employ. Swensen even said:

Even with adequate numbers of high quality personnel, active management strategies demand uninstitutional behavior from institutions, creating a paradox few successfully unravel.

Investing in passively managed vehicles representing individual asset classes effectively eliminates variance from market results. Index funds cost little to implement, present far fewer agency issues than do actively managed portfolios, and promise faithful replication of market portfolios. What explains the fact that few institutional portfolios employ passive management exclusively? Certainly, the game of active management entices players to enter, offering the often false hope of excess returns. Perhaps those few smart enough to recognize that passive strategies provide a superior alternative believe themselves to be smart enough to beat the market. In any event, deviations from benchmark returns represent an important source of portfolio risk.

So in his new book, *Unconventional Success*, Swensen outlined a very simple index fund portfolio for institutions and individuals alike to use as a starting point. The asset allocation looks like this:

30%	Domestic Equity
15%	Foreign Developed Equity
5%	Emerging Market Equity
20%	Real Estate (REITs)
15%	U.S. Treasury Bonds
15%	U.S. Treasury Inflation-Protected Securities (TIPS)

I decided to compared this simple portfolio of low-cost index funds to the more sophisticated approaches used by college endowment funds across the country.

Every year the National Association of College and University Business Officers (NACUBO) puts out a study on the investment performance of a large group college endowment funds. This comprehensive report goes through the asset allocations and performance numbers of funds ranging from a few million dollars to funds with many billions of dollars. In the latest report there were over 800 endowments included in total. Institutional investors are obsessed with peer comparisons so they all eagerly await these performance numbers to see how they stacked up against the competition.

In the hierarchy of institutional investors, you won't find a more competitive group than college endowments. They're in constant competition with not only trying to beat the market, but also beat each other. It's almost like a bizarre finance version of a heated college football or basketball rivalry. Endowment funds try to invest in only the best money managers - utilizing both the public and private markets - to find the very best investment opportunities. They're well-staffed and well-educated. They have access to the best and brightest minds in finance and are able to invest in funds that are reserved only for those with many millions or even billions of dollars.

Here's how Swensen's simple portfolio - which can be purchased for as little as 10 basis points (0.10 percent) from a fund firm like Vanguard - compared to this group of endowment funds:

Annual Performance Results Through June 30, 2015

Size of Endowment	5 year	10 Year
Over $1 Billion	10.4%	7.2%
$501 Million to $1 Billion	9.9%	6.7%
$101 Million to $500 Million	9.5%	6.2%
$51 Million to $100 Million	9.4%	5.9%
$25 Million to $50 Million	9.8%	5.6%
Under $25 Million	10.6%	6.0%
Swensen Index Portfolio	11.6%	8.2%

*Sources: NACUBO/Vanguard

You can see that over the past 5- and 10-year periods, Swensen's simple six index fund portfolio dominated the endowment world's overall performance. Obviously, some endowments did much better (including Yale) but many also did much worse than average.

The point of this exercise is not to advise institutions to invest in this exact portfolio (although it looks like you could do much worse). The point is to show that you don't need a team of PhDs or a huge investment office to earn above-average results. So many institutional investors assume that trying harder will assure them of better results. Unfortunately, trying harder in the markets guarantees nothing and, more often than not, leads to much worse results.

Small and mid-sized institutional investors often find it difficult to gain access to the best fund managers or strategies for a number of reasons. More often than not, the best fund managers in the world have their funds closed to outside investors or require a huge minimum investment to gain access. Therefore, most institutions are left looking for the next best thing; not an easy task to say the least.

Luckily, it's never been easier to access time-tested strategies. Strategies that were once reserved for only the most elite investors are now available to everyone, and the best part is they are now extremely low-cost and efficient to use. Not only are there index funds and ETFs that closely track specific asset classes, sectors or strategies, but there are now also a host of risk factor-based strategies as well.

It turns out that much of what investors formerly saw as alpha or skill can now be explained by a number of different risk factors that can be distilled into simple, low-cost, rules-based strategies. For example, in the past many actively-managed funds outperformed the market by simply buying value stocks, stocks with momentum characteristics or small-cap stocks. These factor strategies are now available in diversified baskets or funds using a systematic approach at a very low cost. For equity strategies these factors include value, momentum, low volatility, quality and shareholder yield. For fixed income strategies these factors include term and credit risk. For hedging strategies, a good example would be trend-following or managed futures.

Active managers would once be labeled as geniuses for outperforming when in reality their skill could be explained by these simple risk factors, which can now be purchased much more cost effectively and packaged more efficiently. Simple ETFs or mutual funds can offer these approaches in a liquid, transparent, low-cost fund structure that wasn't available in the past. At the very least, these funds should be used as a baseline when evaluating current or prospective money managers or fund holdings.

Most institutional investors start with the premise that they need extraordinary results reach their goals before they even attempt to discern those goals and figure out what they actually need. Legendary investor Benjamin Graham once said, "To achieve satisfactory investment results is easier than most people realize; to achieve superior results is harder than it looks."

I'm not saying everyone should index and call it a day. There are certainly actively-managed approaches that can work if you understand them and know what you're getting your fund into. And there are certainly organizations that have the resources, expertise and time to put into the due diligence process when selecting outside managers. But you have to put in the work and you need to have the resolve to stick with it. As a baseline assumption, most institutional investors have to realize that it's difficult to beat a low-cost, low-turnover, long-term oriented approach to investing.

It really comes down to looking yourself in the mirror and understanding where your edge lies and what capabilities you have as an organization. There are many roads to Rome when choosing a portfolio or strategy to implement. Successful funds and organizations are the ones who know what they own, why they own it and then stick with that strategy come hell or high water. The questions board members and investment committees need to ask themselves when considering their investment process are the following:

What asset classes and risk factors do we want or need exposure to?

How do we diversify to minimize unnecessary or avoidable risks?

Is it possible for our consultants to help us pick the best managers or can they help elsewhere?

These questions don't have universal answers and will largely depend on the needs and desires of the organization in question. The last question on consultants is the one we will turn to in the next chapter.

5. CHOOSING AN OUTSOURCED CONSULTANT OR ADVISOR

Here are five questions to consider as you read this chapter:

1. What do we expect from our consultant(s)?
2. Do they offer independent, personal advice, tailored to our specific organizational risks, needs and goals?
3. If we looked out 5-7 years into the future, how would we define this as a successful relationship?
4. How will they help us make better, more informed long-term decisions and help us survive the short to intermediate-term?
5. Will they make our lives easier so we have more time to devote to the mission of the organization?

A survey of American homeowners who had remodeled their kitchens found that they expected to spend, on average, $18,658 on their remodel. Anyone who has ever remodeled their home is cringing right now, because they know that these projects never come in under budget. They actually ended up paying an average of $38,769. Most homeowners are far too optimistic in their own estimations about not only what they will spend, but what their tastes will be once they begin a new project. You could try the do-it-yourself route when making large-scale home improvements, but very few people have the ability or knowhow to start, let alone finish, a huge remodel job on their house. Sure, you could save money in the end going the DIY route, but it would come at the expense of quality or safety from projects gone awry.

This is why most people hire out to a general contractor. The general contractor has a number of roles. They need to make the right recommendations, help people think about things they never even would have considered on their own, set reasonable timelines and goals, monitor the progress and results, implement the plan, stay on budget, ensure quality work is being done, make changes when necessary and hire the right people for each specific aspect of the job. The homeowner still has veto power and has to sign off on all of the decisions to make sure their vision for the project is being heard, but they outsource to professionals where they don't have the required expertise to get the job done.

In a sense this is what many nonprofits are dealing with when deciding on how to manage their portfolios. Some consider the DIY model, but most quickly realize they don't have the time or knowhow to pull it off, so the majority of institutions look to hire their own general contractor in the form of a consultant or advisor.

INTITUTIONAL INVESTMENT CONSULTING

There's an old cartoon that shows a large group of cave men standing around. One says to another, "We have one hunter and one gatherer. Everyone else is a consultant." This same idea could be used to describe many institutional investment programs.

In the U.S., over $13 trillion of institutional capital relies on consultants for investment advice. Pensions, endowments, foundations and other large pools of capital utilize consultants for a wide range of services, most notably due diligence and outside money manager recommendations. Unfortunately, the research shows that investment consultants as a group add no value through their selection of outside investment managers. They chase past performance and make far too many unnecessary changes. Data also shows that the managers consultants fire have gone on to perform better than the ones they hire (as we showed in the previous chapter).

These large pools of capital make the same exact mistakes as mom and pop retail investors, it's just that the reasons tend to be different. Here are a few studies to consider:

- Researchers looked at the investment choices from consulting firms that control roughly 90 percent of the U.S. consulting market. They found, "no evidence that consultants' recommendations add value to plan sponsors." In fact, the average returns were much worse in the funds they recommended than non-recommended funds.
- One study looked at large pension plans, with an average size of $10 billion each. Nearly 600 funds were studied from 1990 to 2011. Researchers found these funds allowed their stock allocation to drift higher during the late-1990s tech bubble. Then they allowed their equity exposure to stay lower at the tail end of the 2007-2009 financial crisis. So they were overweight going into a crash and underweight going into a recovery. Instead of rebalancing they simply chased past performance, thus missing out on the inevitable mean reversion and failed to manage risk according to their stated

guidelines.

- Researchers also looked at the performance of the nation's largest pension plans from 1987 to 1999. Out of the 243 plans in the study, each investing hundreds of millions or even billions of dollars, 90 percent of them failed to beat a simple 60/40 stock/bond portfolio benchmark.
- Another study looked at a dataset of more than 80,000 annual observations of institutional accounts from 1984 through 2007. These funds collectively managed trillions of dollars in assets. The study looked at the buy and sell decisions among stocks, bonds, and externally hired investment managers. The researchers found that the investments that were sold far outperformed the investments that were purchased. Instead of systematically buying low and selling high, these funds bought high and sold low.

One of the problems is that all of these funds end up using the same consultants and investment models. In the U.K., the six largest consultants control 70 percent of the market. In the U.S. the top ten consultants have an 81 percent share. Worldwide, the top ten consulting firms control 82 percent of the market.

If these consultants control so much institutional capital and are considered experts in the field of choosing money managers, why are the results typically so poor?

Consultants constantly feel the need to give as much advice as possible. They have to try to prove that they're worth the fees they charge, so they advise change even when doing nothing is the right move. You can't blame consultants for all of these results and mistakes. Trustees for the funds in question also have to accept a lot of the blame for their decisions and how their investment process affects performance. The short-term performance demands placed on outsourced advisors can create an environment where they feel the need to churn the portfolio or make unnecessary changes. Many consultants are simply giving their clients what they ask for.

Many organizations like having consultants around because it gives them someone else to blame when things go wrong. Institutions can blame the consultants. The consultants can blame the money managers. And the money managers can blame the Fed or some other factor that's out of their control. Everyone is happy except for the end investor, the beneficiaries.

The institutional consulting business model is predicated on scale, which is why the market is so concentrated. But this means that there has to be a herd mentality as all the clients are investing in similar managers and strategies. It also means there is little room for personalized advice when some of these firms are overseeing trillions of dollars in assets. This can lead to something of a cookie-cutter approach to their investment models.

It's costly to perform due diligence and spend time putting clients into smaller money managers, but it's typically these small funds who have a better chance of outperforming since they have a wider opportunity set. Once their outperformance becomes known by the investing community, they are showered with money. Size is the enemy of outperformance in terms of assets under management, but many institutions load up with top performers from the past because they are the funds that have the capacity.

It can be very difficult for these firms to offer objective advice. Consultants typically have a list of approved money managers that they use. It's not very easy for managers to make it onto these lists, but it is very lucrative once they do because that means they will likely be recommended across many different client accounts. The consultant-money manager partnership can be tricky for trustees to understand from a conflict of interest perspective.

Many consultants assume their number one job is to beat the market, provide sources of alpha and help their clients pick the best fund managers. Manager due diligence tends to overshadow tasks such as asset allocation, portfolio construction, performance monitoring, risk management, setting return expectations, educating board members and constantly reminding them how the markets and human nature generally work. The search for alpha often blinds investors from paying attention to the policy basics, which are far more important in the end.

There is so much time wasted debating the relative merits of the different money managers and short-term investment opportunities that it becomes easy to lose sight of your overall goals and organizational mission. Selecting the best investment opportunities won't matter if you can't control your behavior or implement an overarching plan. An investment opportunity should not be confused with an investment process, the latter of which is far more important for those that wish to be successful over the long haul.

DEATH BY A THOUSAND CUTS

Consulting firms can be helpful to institutional investors. They just have to focus on the right areas. The paradox here is that nonprofit institutions need outside advice in most cases. In fact, the Prudent Investor Rule, which is what the fiduciary duty is directly based on, encourages trustees to seek outside help with the management of their portfolio. The problem is they're often paying for the wrong kind of advice.

Warren Buffett seems to agree with me. Here are his thoughts from the 2016 Berkshire Hathaway annual meeting in Omaha:

[T]he consultant has every motivation in the world to tell you, 'this year I think we

should concentrate more on international stocks,' or 'this manager is particularly good on the short side,' and so they come in and they talk for hours, and you pay them a large fee, and they always suggest something other than just sitting on your rear end and participating in the American business without cost. And then those consultants, after they get their fees, they in turn recommend to you other people who charge fees, which… cumulatively eat up capital like crazy.

And the consultants always change their recommendations a little bit from year to year. They can't change them 100% because then it would look like they didn't know what they were doing the year before. So they tweak them from year to year and they come in and they have lots of charts and PowerPoint presentations and they recommend people who are in turn going to charge a lot of money and they say, 'well you can only get the best talent by paying 2-and-20,' or something of the sort, and the flow of money from the 'hyperactive' to what I call the 'helpers' is dramatic.

Like clockwork, every year at nonprofit board meetings across the country consultants pitch a few new fund ideas to replace the current cellar dwellers in the portfolio. No one wants to admit there's a problem with this model of doing business so status quo reigns. It's hard enough to pick one money manager that can outperform, but when you try to pick multiple outperformers and do that multiple times every year your odds just continue to get smaller and smaller. The degree of difficulty is through the roof on this approach.

Here are three consequences of the control the consulting industry has over the institutional investment landscape:

1. As a group, hedge fund performance has been abysmal over the past decade or so. Consultants and those picking the consultants don't receive nearly enough blame for this. The hedge funds are, in most cases, just giving these large institutional investors what they ask for (usually a strategy to fight the last war). Consulting firms pitch their "access" to top performing funds, but that's usually to the funds that outperformed in the past, not to be duplicated in the future.

2. Very few institutions know how to evaluate the consultants who are picking money managers on their behalf, let alone how to perform due diligence on the money managers themselves. Many nonprofits put their faith in their consultants and hope for the best without an understanding of how their picks are really performing.

3. These portfolios end up hurting performance through a death by a thousand cuts. They change a few managers each year. Then they change consultants every few years. Or they change investment committee

members. There's no continuity in their investment approach and each time these changes are implemented there are explicit and implicit costs incurred.

There are many ways in which consultants can add value if they choose to focus their efforts beyond the standard money manager musical chairs:

- Client education and improved communication efforts.
- Behavioral management and modification.
- Performance and risk reporting that doesn't include 100 page reports with useless information no one reads.
- Setting realistic expectations, which can help with both organizational planning needs and keeping investor emotions in check.
- Ensuring the portfolio's asset allocation matches the risk profile and time horizon of the organization.
- Documenting the investment process to ensure continuity in the program over time.
- Saying 'no' over and over again to investments or funds that don't fit within an institution's mandate, tolerance for risk or stated objectives.
- Honesty, transparency and the ability to say "we don't know."
- Reminding these organizations of their time horizons and long-term goals.
- Doing nothing most of the time in terms of making changes to the portfolio.

It's also important - as I'm trying to hammer home in this book over and over again - to ask the right questions. You can't be afraid to speak up when you have concerns or don't fully understand something. A few simple examples to ask current or prospective consultants beyond the typical performance-related queries:

How are you compensated?

What are the all-in, total fees I will be charged?

What's the rationale and evidence behind your approach?

Are there any conflicts of interest at play here?

How do you determine when to make changes to my portfolio or investment plan?

You have to set the correct expectations up front for what you hope to get out of the relationship and then follow-up along the way to make sure the advisor or consultant is doing what they said they were going to do at the outset. All services should be clearly defined up front before coming to an agreement. Some firms only offer money manager due diligence services. Others offer more comprehensive planning and monitoring. Some firms are strictly consultants who act at an arm's length while others take a more hands-on approach and take over much of the day-to-day money management duties. You have to make sure you know what kind of firm you're dealing with upfront, as these things can be confusing to those outside the world of finance.

CONSULTANT OR OUTSOURCED CIO?

In the world of outsourced investment providers, there are typically two different service providers by name - consultants and outsourced chief investment officers ("OCIO"). There are some differences in what each typically provides.

An OCIO is usually hired to act in the same way as if you hired an internal CIO to run your investment office. They are given total discretion to invest within the plan and objectives laid out by the investment committee. The amount of discretion and authority that the committee gives the OCIO varies depending on the firm and organization in question. Some OCIOs simply use model portfolios that all clients are forced to invest in no matter their circumstances. Others firms allow more leeway in terms of personalizing the investments and strategies.

One benefit to this approach is that the OCIO can usually make their own decisions on certain elements in regards to the portfolio without waiting for board approval, which makes for a timelier and efficient portfolio management process. The whole point of outsourcing is to find a firm who has more expertise, time and resources than the investment committee, so it makes sense to give them some slack in terms of implementing their approach.

Most outsourced providers will have a model portfolio or two that they use as a starting point for their long-term institutional clients. There's nothing wrong with using model portfolios as a starting point. But you have to make sure that they are taking all of your needs and objectives into account when placing you into any portfolio allocation.

Consultants, on the other hand, are brought in to make recommendations to a more seasoned investment committee in terms of asset allocation and investment manager or fund selections. The committee still has control over allocation and manager hiring and firing decisions, but they rely on the consultant to help them make better recommendations through the due diligence process. The committee is usually more involved in the process when utilizing a consultant - which can be a good thing or a bad thing depending on the amount of experience the committee has and how much investment knowhow they bring to the table. An inexperienced committee that tries too hard to make too many minor investment decisions is more of a hindrance than a help.

The labels - OCIO, consultant, advisor, coach, etc. - don't matter nearly as much as what services they provide. Regardless of the choice of which type of outsourced services are hired out, the investment committee can never outsource their understanding. They still have to understand the reason for the decisions that are being made. They have to monitor the OCIO or consultant to ensure they are doing exactly what they said they would do. They have to follow a well-reasoned decision-making process when thinking through potential changes or recommendations to the portfolio. Committees have to be aware of their own strengths and weaknesses when delegating to outside firms.

ADDITIONAL SOURCES OF ALPHA

Since traditional investment alpha is getting harder to come by in the financial markets these days, here are four forms of alpha a worthwhile outsourced investment advisor or consultant can provide:

Stress-Relief Alpha. They make your life easier. The majority of the people on boards or committees for nonprofit funds have a lot on their plate. They're focused on other aspects of the organization or even roles with others firms if they are not working directly for the organization in question. Outsourcing the little things can be a huge help.

Decision Alpha. They help you make better, more informed decisions. As we've touched on throughout, the group dynamic can be a tricky one to navigate when trying to make rational decisions. The right advisor will typically be the one who can best manage this process. Providing a better understanding of the difference between a long-term process and short-term outcomes can be one of the hardest ones to figure out and accept as a client, but it's one of the most important aspects of a viable long-term financial relationship. Good consultants can help here.

Crisis Alpha. They help you avoid the big mistake at the worst possible moment. What separates successful investors from those who are unsuccessful is how they handle themselves during severe market disruptions. Having the ability to keep your wits about you and not overreact when markets are falling apart can provide investors with a huge advantage over the competition. The best outsourced investment providers will help stand between you and a huge mistake when things get messy in the markets. There's something of a safety-in-numbers syndrome that occurs during severe bear markets; people feel more comfortable following the herd and making irrational short-term decisions with long-term capital. Most assume that you make all of your money during bull markets, but bear markets are when investors really make or break their performance. Just minimizing mistakes during these periods can put you far ahead of the majority of other investors. Crisis alpha also requires some combination of liquidity, courage and discipline along with a deep understanding of your process and the potential outcomes.

Organizational Alpha. They help you implement better policies and plans. The only way to achieve crisis alpha is by having a detailed plan and process in place to follow so you can understand what to do when bone-crushing volatility inevitably hits the markets. This requires a documented investment plan with specific checks and balances in place so you can lay out a plan of attack before your emotions come into play. If your consultant can't help your organization improve in the planning or process department they probably aren't going to be helpful for very long. This is where they can really earn their keep. Building a portfolio, choosing the correct funds or securities, searching for investment opportunities - none of these things will matter if you don't have an effective mechanism in place for making rational decisions during irrational markets. This includes a deep understanding of your true tolerance for risk, various time horizons, goals and investment philosophy.

Organization alpha can include, but is not limited to:

- Helping the organization set realistic objectives and expectations.
- Providing guidance on asset allocation, investment restrictions, investment recommendations and fee reviews.
- Negotiating custodial agreements and fees.
- Liability and asset allocation studies.
- Implementation of the investment strategy.
- Recommending changes to the portfolio or plan.
- Providing oversight towards the goals of the organization.
- Cash management and spending policy guidance.

You'll notice nowhere in this list did I mention historical performance or track records. That's because historical performance, especially of the short-term variety, is fairly meaningless. If your goal is to find a consultant or OCIO to help your investments outperform "the market" then you've probably already lost. The four Ps of due diligence are people, process, portfolio and performance. Focus all of your time and attention on the first three Ps and the fourth one will take care of itself.

In the next chapter, we'll take a look at alternative investments and see if they can help investors improve their performance.

6. ALTERNATIVE INVESTMENTS

Here are five questions to consider as you read this chapter:

1. Do we have the right type of organization to invest in alternative investments?
2. Do we need alternative investments to reach our goals?
3. Do we understand how these investments typically work?
4. Do we understand the risks involved with alternative investments?
5. Can we consistently pick the best managers who can overcome the high costs involved with alternatives?

Hedge funds are a lightning rod in the financial industry. The most vocal critics and proponents both offer extreme views that paint a very different picture on the same topic. Some will bash hedge funds no matter what while others will rush to their defense anytime they're criticized. The recent poor returns in hedge funds coupled with the high fees they charge are a big reason for the criticism.

On the one hand, you have the critics who can't seem to understand why anyone would ever invest money in a group of funds that have collectively failed to beat a simple 60/40 stock-bond mix every single year since 2002 while also charging outrageous fees and locking up investor capital in an illiquid fund structure. According to a recent study that analyzed the returns of U.S. pension funds from 1998-2014, hedge funds provided a lower annual return than every asset class outside of cash.

On the other hand, you have proponents who work for or invest in hedge funds that point to the long-term track records of such legendary hedge fund managers as Stanley Druckenmiller, George Soros, Ray Dalio, Seth Klarman, Daniel Loeb, Jim Simons and others who have had enormous success in the markets and built vast sums of wealth because of it.

I want to give a more nuanced, less biased point of view as someone who has invested in a number of hedge funds over the years and witnessed firsthand the good, the bad and the ugly that these types of investments have to offer. I have some thoughts on why these funds have run into so

48

much trouble and scrutiny over the past decade or so based on my experience in the hedge fund world.

Here goes...

The Institutionalization of Hedge Funds. Once the pensions, sovereign wealth funds, endowments, foundations and family offices made it a point to invest in hedge funds it became obvious that the entire industry would become institutionalized. According to Citigroup, institutional investors currently account for 71% of hedge fund assets, versus just 20% in 2002. Because of this the due diligence is now so focused on operational and organizational risk that the investment process almost becomes secondary. The biggest hedge funds are today's version of the Nifty Fifty one-decision stocks from the 1960s and 1970s. They have fully-staffed back offices, hundreds of PhDs and the best lawyers in the business who are able to craft a three-hundred-page prospectus that frees the fund from any potential litigation risk. The large nonprofit investors tend to invest most of their money in these large, "safe" funds.

Narratives are Constantly Changing. Institutionalization has also changed the way most funds invest as expectations have shifted. Back in the heyday of George Soros and Michael Steinhardt in the 1970s and 1980s, hedge fund managers were mostly looking for home-run returns. It was something of a Wild West in terms of how they operated. As more institutions began to allocate to hedge funds the narrative shifted from the managers who tried to knock it out of the park in any type of environment to stock-like returns with bond-like volatility. Value investing staged a huge comeback following the dot-com crash, so fundamental long/short managers did very well by going long cheap stocks and short expensive stocks. This really increased interest in hedge funds and led to an explosion in the number of funds available.

After seeing solid returns during a bear market, investor interest shifted into these long/short funds which next morphed into downside volatility protection and global macro funds following the Great Recession. The goal now seems to be that institutions want hedge funds to simply avoid any and all headline risk or volatility, while earning a steady annual return stream.

This narrative shift is a classic performance chase by both investors and portfolio managers alike. Both sides are to blame here. Investors are always fighting the last war and hedge funds are more than willing to oblige if it means more assets under management. This is an over-generalization, but it's definitely a factor for much of the hedge fund industry today as both sides understand how career risk works.

"Hedge Fund" is a Misnomer. Everyone wants to make hedge funds an asset class. That's not the case. Hedge funds are a fund structure, not an asset class. There are so many different types of hedge funds that it's becoming difficult to keep track. You have long/short, market neutral, managed futures, activist, credit, stat-arb, merger arb, special situations, distressed debt, short bias, event-driven, macro and probably a few others I'm sure I've missed. Then there are multi-strategy funds and fund of funds; and this doesn't even break things down by geography, specialty or sectors. The options and combinations are nearly endless. And the institutionalization of the industry means that most large allocators are trying to pick one of each fund type in something of a hedge fund style box, which is a great way to achieve mediocre returns.

Plus, most funds aren't really hedging in the way most people use the term. They're not all market neutral funds that hedge out all market exposure. Most hedge funds are making directional bets when they go short, not hedging risks in the portfolio. I'm not sure many hedge fund investors realize this.

Increased Competition. It's insane how many hedge funds there are these days. At my old job we would probably receive dozens of cold calls or email sales pitches a week from various hedge funds. I was always amazed at: (a) the number of funds that managed hundreds of millions or even billions of dollars that I had never heard of before; and (b) the number of new funds that popped up out of the blue on a regular basis, usually founded by people who were going out on their own from an established fund or bank prop trading desk.

There used to be a few hundred million dollars in hedge funds; now it's a few trillion. As the best funds build impressive track records, money piles in from all corners, which only makes it that much more difficult to keep up the outperformance with more money to manage. And, as technology improves, it's becoming much easier for algorithms to do the work that was once branded as differentiation by portfolio managers. As we discussed earlier in the book, this shrinks the alpha available to all of these funds.

The Yale Model. Every other institutional fund in the world looked at what David Swensen was able to do at Yale and assumed that it would be simple to recreate his due diligence process and pick top-flight managers. Not only are there fewer opportunities for alpha available because there are 10,000 plus hedge funds in the world, but there are also tens of thousands of institutional and high-net worth asset allocators who are competing for access to the very best funds with the likes of Yale. There's just not enough top flight funds to go around. And while Yale has access to pretty much any fund they want, it's not so easy for others to invest with the best of the best. Most of them don't want your money because they already have enough capital at their disposal.

Fees. This is an easy point of contention for critics to point to, but it's definitely a huge factor when combined with the over-saturation of funds charging the same high rates. Once you factor in the performance incentive in the 2&20 fee structure (which is probably closer to 1.5&17.5 now) it works out to a 4 to 5 percent annual fee in total. That's a huge hurdle rate and doesn't even include the costs of trading or the due diligence costs that investors are putting into vetting these funds. I don't know what the correct fee structure should be for hedge funds, but with costs coming down everywhere else in the fund industry, 95 percent of these funds have no business charging what they do.

Probabilities. Legendary hedge fund manager Ray Dalio once described hedge funds by saying, "There are about 8,000 planes in the air and 100 really good pilots." That's probably pushing it, but it's likely not too far off. An executive from institutional consultant Cambridge Associates recently stated that roughly 5 percent percent of the 10,000 or so hedge funds merit institutional investment. That would mean that 95 percent do not.

I know for a fact that there are many really great portfolio managers and teams out there running hedge funds. I've seen the track records first hand. Some of the performance numbers in both good and bad markets are nothing short of amazing. That consistency is one of the things that draws investor attention to these funds.

But, if there are only a small number of hedge funds that are worth the high fees, then there is an even smaller number of fund investors that are able to: (a) identify the best funds in advance; (b) gain access to these funds; or (c) know when it's time to exit an underperforming or oversubscribed fund. My guess is the majority of institutional and individual investors in hedge funds don't really understand the strategies they're investing in. This lack of understanding has led to unrealistic expectations in what funds can (and cannot) do for their investors.

I'm not saying it's impossible, but there are very few teams or individuals who can put in the work to build and maintain a viable hedge fund allocation. Nor am I saying all hedge funds are terrible. It's just that there is a huge gap between the top funds and everyone else. This means investors are constantly trying to pick up-and-coming fund managers, which is probably even harder than identifying those who will stay on top.

WHY PEOPLE INVEST IN HEDGE FUNDS

If it's so hard to pick the right hedge funds, why are there so many investors in this space? What fascinates me most about the investment business is how incentives and human nature drive people's decisions. Here are a few thoughts as to why so many investors are now invested in hedge funds:

Most Hedge Fund Managers are Brilliant. These people don't raise millions or even billions of dollars without having a high level of intelligence. When you meet face-to-face with the best hedge fund managers it's almost impossible to walk away unimpressed. Most of the best funds have made it so you almost feel entitled or lucky to be handing over your money to them. That's how good some of these managers are at persuading people of their brilliance. Some people will never be able to resist the charm of intelligence and charisma.

It Looks Like a Smart Move to a Board of Directors. I'm always amazed at how much people underestimate the role of career risk in the investment industry. It could be one of the biggest inefficiencies in the markets when you consider how much money professional investors collectively manage. Keep things too simple and you're the only one to blame when things go wrong.

Non-correlated returns, stock-like returns with bond-like volatility, upside participation with limited downside risk and alpha generation all sound very impressive when you have to answer to the board that oversees your institutional fund. If nothing else, hedge funds are interesting. That narrative is very appealing to certain groups of investors.

They Have the Best Sales and Marketing Teams. With high fees come plenty of resources to hire the best and brightest to build your support staff. Not only are the portfolio managers interesting to talk to, but the people who manage the relationships for these funds are the best in the business. They have the sales and marketing process perfected better than anyone.

There's Always a Good Time to Invest. This is true with any money manager, but hedge funds have turned this idea into an art form. In the aftermath of the crash we were told we had to invest with them because, "Look what just happened...," playing up to people's recency bias. And, following the bull market, we were told we had to invest with them because, "Another crash is on the way..." They're very good at preying on investor fears to raise capital and fear sells.

It's a Status Symbol. I was sitting in on a panel at a conference a number of years ago with a handful of mid-sized endowments and foundations. These funds had a few hundred million dollars compared to the billions managed by everyone else in the room. One CIO told the crowd that his fund "only" had 20 percent of their fund allocated to alternatives, like hedge funds. But he was quick to point out that the allocation would certainly grow in the coming years. It was like he was ashamed that his organization's portfolio didn't have 50 to 70 percent in alts like everyone else (pretty standard these days for larger funds). Peer pressure and the status symbol of creating a "sophisticated" portfolio is a real issue for many of these organizations, whether they're willing to admit it or not.

Follow the Leader. Consultants, advisors, family offices and institutional investors are constantly looking at best practices to keep up with the rest of the industry. On the institutional side of the business there is plenty of peer-to-peer sharing of manager recommendations and due diligence that goes on because no one wants to be surprised by a lack of information. Everyone likes to think they're a contrarian in this business, but it always feels much safer to go with the herd and do what everyone else is doing. Hedge funds are a perfect example of this as the large allocators of capital typically all invest in the same or similar funds.

Emerging Managers. Every year there are a few emerging hedge fund managers that come out of nowhere and shoot the lights out with their performance. If you can find these emerging funds before everyone else does, the returns can be spectacular. As with most things, this is easier said than done. I've seen many emerging manager fund-of-funds crash and burn. Even though their entire line of business is predicated on finding the diamonds in the rough, it's a tall task when trying to pick the next George Soros.

The Holy Grail in this space is the fund manager who doesn't want to become institutionalized and is content managing money for a small number of investors and never wants to get too big. It's very rare, but I've seen a handful of these types of funds.

Track Records. It's not like it's all smoke and mirrors. Some people out there seem to assume that rich people and institutional investors really just like shoveling money into the furnace by paying 2&20 to underperforming hedge funds. There are great funds out there, but the chances that you are going to have access to them is slim to none. Yet, hope springs eternal.

Ego. Most big investors are unwilling to admit that they'll never be able to invest in this small group of outperforming funds or pick the best emerging managers, but that doesn't stop them from trying.

Sure it's a tough business for everyone else, but we have the best due diligence process in the industry. We have all the right connections. Our access is unprecedented. We only invest in top quartile managers. It's everyone else that picks the bottom of the barrel funds.

It's amazing how many people assume they only invest in the top echelon of funds. It makes you wonder who all these suckers are investing in the rest of funds out there. It has to be someone. The fact remains that the majority of investors in hedge funds are ill-equipped to invest in this space. Most people have been, or will be, disappointed by their hedge fund investments. One of the biggest reasons for this is that they don't know why they've invested in them in the first place.

ALTERNATIVES ON TOP OF ALTERNATIVES

There's nothing special about alternative investments. Really they are just investment structures that allow investors to utilize leverage, invest in private assets, short (bet against) securities or invest in non-traditional investment styles. They are still invested in equities, fixed income and commodities; they just do so in different ways than the more traditional route.

The pros of this approach include the possibility for higher risk-adjusted returns that are uncorrelated to the broader stock and bond markets. The cons include higher fees, increased due diligence and monitoring costs, illiquidity and the fact that it's difficult to pick or gain access to the very best fund offerings.

As we touched on earlier in the book, one of the reasons it's getting so hard to pick the winners is simply because there is more competition than ever for those looking to manage your money. Private investments have quietly exploded in size over the past few years. In addition to the 10,000 or so hedge funds in existence, according to the SEC, there are also:

8,407	Private Equity Funds
4,058	"Other" Private Funds
2,386	Section 4 Private Equity Funds
1,789	Real Estate Funds
1,327	Securitized Asset Funds
504	Venture Capital Funds

So why are we seeing such enormous growth in the private markets? There's the fact that you can charge much higher fees in an alternative investment fund structure, so the talent has migrated there in hopes of earning more money. If you really want to understand why something is happening, follow the incentives. Part of it has to do with the low interest-rate environment we've been in since the financial crisis. Competition among investors is so fierce these days that allocators of capital are looking for outperformance anywhere they can find it. Giant pension and sovereign wealth funds have also made more investments in hedge funds and private equity over the past decade or so, because they would like to increase their return expectations.

Whether these higher returns materialize is another matter altogether, but I do think that there are a number of unintended consequences from this push by institutional investors into alternatives:

Fraud. It's much easier to defraud your investors in a private fund structure. In *The Hedge Fund Mirage*, Simon Lack says, "If you want to defraud people, a slightly mysterious trading strategy with an apparent strong history of performance in an LP [Limited Partnership] structure generally outside the regulatory framework is one of the best ways to do it." My sense is most of the due diligence on these types of fund structures is severely lacking and most don't really understand what they're getting themselves into. We could certainly see larger investors getting swindled in the years ahead because of it.

Liquidity. A number of very large institutional funds got burned by having too much exposure to private fund structures during the financial crisis and not enough liquidity to meet short-term needs. You would assume these issues would have caused these large allocators of capital to re-think their investments in this area. Instead, many have doubled down and only increased their allocations to LP fund structures. I'm curious to see how the funds with heavy alternative exposure survive the next downturn with such an illiquid profile. Hopefully they've all learned their lesson, but I'm dubious.

Painful Transition Periods. Harvard's endowment fund is on its sixth CIO (chief investment officer) in the past decade. One of the reasons the new people stepping in have had such a hard time is because they've all been dealing with legacy assets from the previous CIOs. Private investments are typically invested over a period that can range anywhere from 1-15 years. The distribution phase can last just as long. Once you're locked up in these funds it's very difficult to get out unless you sell on the secondary market for pennies on the dollar. It becomes nearly impossible to have any continuity in your investment plan once someone else steps in and tries to make changes.

Operational Headaches. The majority of investors don't have the requisite due diligence processes in place to be able to thoroughly vet or monitor these types of investments. It really is a full time job that requires a ton of work. Not only that, but they can be a nightmare from an operational standpoint if you don't have the back office in place to deal with auditors, handle the cash flows, figure out the marks on the investments and understand how to track and measure the performance. There aren't many rules of thumb or industry standards in this space.

The rallying cry for investing in private markets has always been that they're inefficient and offer investors an illiquidity premium. This is true for the top 5 percent or so of funds that have built-in competitive advantages. For everyone else in this space the competition means fewer opportunities for outperformance and the potential for higher risks to potentially get there.

Plus, many of institutional investors hold anywhere from 20 to 100 separate funds in their portfolios. The due diligence and monitoring costs necessary for a portfolio with this many money managers can be enormous. Not very many funds, even at the institutional level, have the operational capabilities or available staff to oversee that many managers or funds.

This approach of using tens or even hundreds of different funds can also lead to a form of phony diversification. Diversification only works if you're able to understand how the different portfolio components fit together and complement one another. It would be nearly impossible to understand your portfolio exposures and manage risk when utilizing so many different money managers. It's difficult to estimate these costs of complexity, but they make for an inefficient investment program in the wrong hands.

The main reason many investors have performed so poorly using alternative investments is because they don't understand there's a huge difference between traditional and alternative investments in terms of portfolio management and construction. It's not necessarily that the funds themselves have performed poorly (although many have); it's how they're being used in an overall portfolio construct that's the issue.

With traditional investments:

- Diversification is one of the few free lunches that exists in the markets. It allows you to increase your long-term risk-adjusted returns by adding additional assets together.
- Diversification by geography, asset class, market cap and strategy can improve results.
- Average returns will almost certainly lead to above-average results in terms of your peers, because index returns beat the majority of actively managed funds (as we saw in Chapter 4).

With alternative investments:

- Diversification almost ensures that you will see sub-par results.

- Diversification by vintage year, buyout size/type and hedge fund strategy/style can actually hurt your results when it's done in the style box fashion of traditional portfolio management.
- Average returns will most likely lead to below-average market results (especially in hedge funds).

Take a look at this data from one of Yale's Endowment reports that illustrates the huge dispersion in results for a number of traditional and alternative asset classes:

Spread Between Top & Bottom Quartile Manager Performance	Asset Class
0.5%	U.S. Bonds
1.9%	U.S. Stocks
4.0%	Foreign Stocks
4.8%	Small Cap Stocks
7.1%	Hedge Funds
13.7%	Private Equity
43.2%	Venture Capital

This data looks at the ten year performance numbers for all money managers in each specific asset class and then subtracts the top 25% of performers from the bottom 25% of performers. The spread is really showing how wide or narrow the returns are between the best and worst performing money managers in each respective asset class. For instance, there wasn't a huge dispersion between the top and bottom quartile performers for U.S. stock money managers (less than 2 percent between the top and bottom), but there was a huge dispersion between the top and bottom quartiles in venture capital performance (nearly 45 percent!). So there isn't much room for over- or under-performance in U.S. bond funds, U.S. stock funds or foreign stock funds, but there is a huge margin for error in hedge funds, private equity and venture capital. What this tells you is that if you are going to try your hand in alternative investments, you better make sure you're able to both pick and gain access to the top quartile funds in these segments, because the fall-off is immense if you're wrong.

These results were for the ten years ending in 2005, but Yale performed the same study for their 2013 Endowment Report, which showed similar results. There isn't a huge performance difference between the top- and bottom-performing asset managers in stocks and bonds, but within alternatives there is a huge difference between the top- and bottom-performers. The more managers you add to this space, the easier it becomes to pick a poor-performing fund. Over-diversification can increase your risks of sub-par performance because you increase your odds of picking a fund manager who blows up. With traditional investments you more or less know what you're getting yourself into. This is not so with alternatives, especially if you don't have the necessary background required to understand these more complex investment strategies.

I understand why so many institutional funds manage their portfolios this way. The high dispersion in alternative manager performance leads to a huge concentration risk if you pick the wrong fund. And alts have a much higher blow-up potential because they utilize leverage and illiquid securities. Therefore, most investors aren't comfortable investing in just a few select fund managers or strategies. So there's a double-edged sword of the desire for diversification on the one hand and the problem with too much diversification on the other.

I'm not saying it can't be done, but in many ways this is a form of 'threading the needle' in investment management. As David Swensen said in that very same Yale report:

Selecting top managers in private markets leads to much greater reward than identifying top managers in public markets. On the other hand, poor private manager selection can lead to extremely disappointing results as a consequence of high fees, poor performance, and illiquid positions.

The margin for error is much higher in alternatives. If you're going to go this route, my sense is it would work best by pairing traditional investments with a select few alternative managers. It's not an easy solution by any means, but outperforming is not easy in this space. The problem is everyone assumes they can consistently pick top quartile funds from a combination of hope, hubris and overconfidence.

OPERATIONAL EFFICIENCY

One of the most overlooked aspects of portfolio management is the time constraint that your investments can place on your organization. Operational efficiency can play a large role is helping institutions make better, more informed decisions. Operationally inefficient investment programs can miss the forest for the trees by constantly getting bogged down in the minutiae. There is much more that goes into investing in alternatives beyond talking to portfolio managers and picking a strategy. The due diligence is just the first step. Implementation and monitoring can be even more time consuming and confusing for those who aren't experts in the field.

First of all, the legal paperwork for the subscription documents and private placement memorandums (PPMs) for these funds can be overwhelming. We're talking 100-200 page documents galore. And the hedge funds and private equity managers have some of the best lawyers in the business (because they can afford it) who are able to make these documents basically indecipherable, save for those who know exactly what they're looking at. It's basically a requirement these days to have a lawyer on staff who knows the legal ins and outs of these documents when performing due diligence before signing on the bottom line to make an investment.

Making contributions to hedge funds is easy (assuming you can get into the funds you want to invest with). You can typically invest on a monthly or quarterly basis without much notice. But try getting your money out and it could be a different story. Most funds require at least 90 days' notice and even then you can only redeem on a quarterly or annual basis in most cases. Some funds have lock-up periods that last even longer, anywhere from to 180 days to 3 years.

If you decide to cut ties with the fund altogether and redeem all of your capital you typically only get 80 to 90 percent of your money back from the hedge fund at redemption. The other 10 to 20 percent "holdback" doesn't get returned to you until the hedge fund's annual audit which could be up to a year later. So you are forced to sit and wait as your money earns nothing while they make sure the net asset value (NAV) of the fund is correct as it was reported. Contrast this with stocks, mutual funds and ETFs that are priced every second of the trading day.

If your hedge fund closes for any reason, you get a much better sense of what's lurking under the surface in terms of illiquid holdings. Hedge funds can close because of the loss of large investors, untimely investments or simply managers who become bored with the process because they have more than enough money and are sick of dealing with unrealistic client expectations. These fund closures can take much longer than you would imagine and can lead to a huge opportunity cost of your capital. Fund unwinds can take months or even years in some cases, depending on the size and types of assets in question.

Private equity investments also come with huge opportunity costs. You don't simply hand over the amount you commit to a fund on day one and start investing. With extensions, the investment period could last up to 10-15 years. So you have to figure out how to manage liquidity in the meantime as the funds slowly call their capital over time for their various investments. This can make it very difficult to stay within your stated asset allocation policy guidelines when you don't know the timing, or the size of the cash flows that will eventually be called in by the managers when they decide to put money to work. There's no set schedule; every fund and investing environment is different.

Private equity fees are a sweet deal for the managers, too. With the majority of funds, you don't pay management fees on your invested capital.

You actually pay on your committed capital. So if you have $30 million committed to a private equity fund, but they only call $500,000 in year one, your 2 percent annual management fee (paid on $30 million) is over 100 percent of invested capital.

PRIVATE EQUITY CHALLENGES

It can also be difficult to understand exactly how well your private equity funds are really performing when monitoring the results. Here are a few caveats that rarely get mentioned when discussing private equity returns:

IRRs are Not Compounded Returns. Since private equity investments are often make sporadically over time, funds tend to report IRRs to their investors for performance purposes. There's nothing wrong with reporting performance numbers this way, but there's a huge difference between an internal rate of return ("IRR") and a compounded rate of return (which is how investors are used to seeing their results from traditional investments). IRRs tell you how well the investor did with the capital they employed, but not how much of the capital was used. An IRR can be a very misleading return number if you don't understand how to read it correctly.

Cash Flow Magnitude Matters. Let's say your pension fund makes a $10 million commitment to a private equity fund. It's highly likely that just $6-$7 million of that capital will ever be invested by the private equity fund over the life of the investment period. This is because, on average, private equity funds only call roughly 60 to 70 percent of committed capital. This means that while investors may be receiving decent returns on their private investments, it's being earned on a smaller capital base than they may realize, thus diminishing the impact of the returns on the overall portfolio.

The Timing of the Cash Flows Matter. When our hypothetical pension fund makes its $10 million commitment to a private equity fund, they don't simply hand over that money all at once. It gets invested as opportunities arise. The investment period can last a number of years. But the IRR stat places a lot of weight on the earliest cash flows. When you invest, and how quickly you get your money back, can have a huge impact on the IRR calculation. Short-term successes and failures can distort IRRs and don't always tell the whole story. IRRs also don't take into account the opportunity cost of sitting in cash or other investments for a number of years as investors wait to have their capital deployed by PE firms.

Benchmarking is Difficult. A number that far too few investors or funds use is a multiple of capital. A 2x multiple would mean that an investor in a fund doubled their money (although, to be fair, venture capital funds pay more attention to these numbers). The multiple of capital approach is much more tangible than an IRR. Also, when making private-to-public market comparisons, many private equity funds use a constant public market index, such as annual S&P 500 returns. A more apples-to-apples comparison would examine private investments and public investments on a cash-flow weighted basis as private investments are made periodically. So, it would look at how that investment would have done in the stock market during the same time frame the cash was put to work. It levels the playing field, so to speak. And this doesn't even take into consideration the leverage or illiquidity involved in private equity, another risk to consider.

Because of all of these issues, there really are no standards in the institutional investment world to account for private equity returns in a portfolio. Compounded returns would probably understate performance, while IRRs may overstate it. The numbers you see from most PE firms and institutional investors alike are not what they appear to be at first glance.

Swensen has earned unbelievably returns in private equity, but he cautions investors on this space:

Buyout funds constitute a poor investment for casual investors. The underlying company investments in buyout funds differ from their public market counterparts only in degree of balance sheet risk and in degree of liquidity. The higher debt and the lower liquidity of buyout deals demand higher compensation in the form of superior returns to investors. Unfortunately, for private equity investors, in recent decades buyout funds delivered lower returns than comparable marketable securities positions, even before adjusting for risk.

As with other forms of investments that depend on superior active management, sensible investors look at buyout partnerships with a high degree of skepticism. Unless investors command the resources necessary to identify top-quartile or even top-decile managers, results almost certainly fail to compensate for the degree of risk incurred.

Investors are often far too believing of statistics without placing them in the correct context. Swensen also discussed this in terms of hedge fund returns as well:

Statistics on the past performance of hedge funds fail to provide much insight into the character of this relatively new segment of the investment world. Survivorship bias presents a pervasive problem for gatherers of historical return data. The fact that poorly performing firms fail at higher rates than well-performing firms causes data on manager returns to overstate past results, since compilations of data at any point in time from the current group of managers inevitably lack complete performance numbers from firms that failed in the past. In the well-established, comprehensively documented world of traditional marketable securities, survivorship bias presents a significant, albeit quantifiable problem. In the less well-established, less comprehensively documented arena of hedge fund investing, survivorship bias creates a much more substantial informational challenge.

Don't believe everything you read or see in terms of performance numbers for these funds. And echoing Swensen's sentiments, if you're a casual investor in this space you're asking for poor results.

THERE IS NO SECRET RECIPE

A researcher from Columbia University studied endowment funds of various sizes in terms of their performance and asset allocation decisions to get a handle on what sets the top performing funds apart from everyone else. He found that the large Ivy League endowments, such as Yale, University of Pennsylvania, Columbia, etc. had the best performing funds. But his conclusion didn't state that these larger institutions were smarter or more sophisticated than their smaller peers; it's just that they took more risk in their portfolios to earn higher returns. The study's author, David Chen, concluded, "There is no secret recipe for outperformers. The higher return of bigger endowments can be attributed to risk compensation rather than to an informational premium."

You can see this in action by looking at the average asset allocation of the different college endowments and foundations by the size of their assets:

Asset Allocations for U.S. College & University Endowments & Foundations, Fiscal Year 2015

Size of Endowment	Domestic Equities	Fixed Income	International Equities	Alternative Strategies	Short-Term/ Cash/Other
Over $1 Billion	13%	7%	19%	57%	4%
$501 Million to $1 Billion	21%	9%	20%	44%	6%
$101 Million to $500 Million	27%	13%	21%	34%	5%
$51 Million to $100 Million	33%	17%	20%	25%	5%
$25 Million to $50 Million	40%	20%	18%	16%	6%
Under $25 Million	42%	24%	15%	11%	8%

Source: NACUBO

The larger funds are willing and able to take more risk (alternative strategies have similar or higher risk profiles than equities) and those are the funds that have generally enjoyed the higher than average returns over the years. You can tell simply by looking at the asset allocations in this chart why this would be the case over the long-term. These funds have fewer assets in bonds or fixed-income investments; thus, there is more of a bias towards equity investments, which have a higher expected return over time.

Much of this is likely driven by the how these organizations are structured. These endowments often have a large, wealthy donor base along with enormous assets under management and funds that are set up to last perpetually (a big word for forever). This allows them to take greater risk with their assets. The smaller and mid-sized institutions either don't have the ability or the willingness to take more risk because they can't stomach the short-term pain you must deal with to earn decent long-term gains in the markets.

Risk and return are attached at the hip in the capital markets. To earn a higher return in the long-run you must be willing to accept a higher probability for short-term losses and volatility. Chen continued in his paper that, "People are willing to bear more risk in investments once they become richer," and concluded, "this is consistent with the empirical finding in this paper that higher capital return comes from more risk."

This all comes back to the most important attribute of successful investing: know thyself. If your organization can't accept more risk to see those higher expected returns, you can't beat yourself up about lagging your larger, more established peers in the institutional investment world. But, if your organization does have the ability to accept more risk, then it's on you to ensure that you're able to earn organizational alpha by setting up policies and guidelines that allow for a successful long-term investment program.

One of the best ways to do this is by having the correct policies and plans in the first place. In the next chapter, we'll look at how to structure successful investment policy.

7. INVESTMENT POLICY

Here are five questions to consider as you read this chapter:

1. Do we have a comprehensive investment policy statement ("IPS") in place that we can both follow and understand?
2. Do we have an investment committee charter that outlines our duties and responsibilities?
3. Do we have documented spending policies and cash management guidelines in place to plan for liquidity events?
4. Have we documented all policies, guidelines, contingencies and plans to ensure continuity in our investment program?
5. Will we have the courage and discipline to follow our plan even when it's painful to do so?

In the U.S. there are close to six million commercial buildings with a collective eighty-seven billion square feet of floor space. There are also over one hundred million low rise homes and almost ten million more high rises.

The complexity required to build a skyscraper, residential home or commercial building is off the charts. You have to consider building codes, height requirements, the wants and needs of the clients, the makeup of the ground you're building on, the materials, the design, the engineering and the size of the project. And then you have to turn those designs and plans into an actual building structure by dealing with various tools, machines, workers and projects. You also have to finish everything in the correct order, all while dealing with problems and unavoidable complexities along the way.

Yet somehow the failure rate for commercial buildings - defined as a partial or full collapse of a working building structure - is tiny, at just 0.00002 percent per year. And builders can now finish a building in a third less time than they could just 2-3 decades ago, even though they are now dealing with tougher codes and building standards.

So why is this the case?

According to Dr. Atul Gawande in his book, *The Checklist Manifesto:*

How to Get Things Right, the way to navigate a complex situation such as this is by documenting your process with the use of thorough communication along the way. As the title of his book would suggest, Dr. Gawande is a huge proponent of checklists. Here he explains:

> *It is unnerving to think that we allow buildings this difficult to design and construct to go up in the midst of our major cities, with thousands of people inside and tens of thousands more living and working nearby. Doing so seems risky and unwise. But we allow it based on trust in the ability of the experts to manage the complexities. They in turn know better than to rely on their individual abilities to get everything right. They trust instead in one set of checklists to make sure that simple steps are not missed or skipped and in another set to make sure that everyone talks through and resolves all the hard and unexpected problems.*

He continues:

> *Checklists seem able to defend anyone, even the experienced, against failure in many more tasks than we realized. They provide a kind of cognitive net. They catch mental flaws inherent in all of us - flaws of memory and attention and thoroughness. And because they do, they raise wide, unexpected possibilities.*

Dr. Gawande goes on to explain that checklists can help in a number of different professions. Doctors, surgeons, builders and airline pilots have all experienced huge improvements in their respective fields by decreasing their number of mistakes through the use of checklists.

In many ways building a well-functioning investment program can be a lot like building a skyscraper. You have to understand building codes and regulations (investment policies and guidelines). You have a lay a good foundation (asset allocation). You have to erect a sturdy frame (risk management and portfolio construction). Then you have to put your own individual touches on it to make it your own (individual investment strategies and holdings). And finally the real fun begins once you have to see things through and build the structure to match the specifications of the plan (follow and implement your investment plan).

In this final chapter of the book I'm going to go through something of an institutional investor checklist, but first I'd like to discuss why governance is so important in the institutional space and what investors, allocators, trustees and board members need to know when thinking about it.

GOVERNANCE

Too much time in the investment industry is spent focused on areas where investors or clients have little-to-no control. Investors are all so preoccupied by noise - central banks, economic growth, interest rates, tax rates, inflation, government policy and the actions of politicians - that it can drown out the truly important variable that are less sexy, but far more important. There is also an inordinate amount of time and money devoted to the search for the best investment opportunities or the top-performing money managers. Everyone is concerned with track records, past performance, alpha and peer rankings. Very little time is spent on the one focal point that everyone can use to improve their results - policy.

There are so many hard-working, intelligent people who spend their time trying to beat the market that the competition is nearly insurmountable for all but a few who have the brains, wisdom, connections and courage to succeed. But market-beating performance is promised to no one. The main focus should instead rely on what you can control - namely determining your needs, setting reasonable goals and allocating your portfolio to create a high probability for success.

Ensuring a high probability for success will always start with sound investment policy. These policies can help organizations document their specific financial details, objectives, guidelines, risks, fears and long-term goals. Financial professionals and investors are focusing more of their time on short-term events than ever before, while time horizons continue to lengthen for most investors as people continue to live longer. That's why policy is so important because it allows you to ignore the short-term noise and focus on your actual long-term strengths and weaknesses as an organization.

As we talked about in Chapter 5, for most organizations, it's going to make sense to outsource some facets of the portfolio management process. But you can't completely outsource the right investment policy. No one knows an organization's mission, needs and desires better than the employees and board members working on its behalf. You have to understand your financial situation, define your various goals and objectives, have an understanding of your limitations and outline your investment philosophy. You can have the best consultant, advisor, funds or portfolio managers in the world, but those hires will be all for naught without the requisite emotional checks and balances in place to ensure that you're able to follow through with your original plan.

It's not alpha, beta or Sharpe ratios that will determine your success in the markets, but how well you're able to control your fear, greed, envy and ever-changing perception of risk. Having the resolve to follow a plan has more to do with your investment performance than any economic or market prognostication. You have to remain committed to the process and continue to learn as you go. You have to understand probabilities and statistics when making plans about an uncertain future. You must have an understanding of financial market history, how various investments typically behave, and the potential risks involved.

A study of historical booms and busts is a good starting point. Human nature is such that the pendulum will always swing too far in either direction between extreme euphoria and brutal pessimism from investors. However, knowledge alone won't be enough if you don't have the discipline to implement a plan and faithfully follow it when times get tough. If you're unable to stay the course and practice benign neglect with your portfolio the majority of the time it's going to be tough to be successful.

Governance goes beyond portfolio management and performance. It starts with being able to articulate the organization's long-term goals and unique financial situation and needs. You have to perform a thorough review of the organization's resources and capabilities. This includes finding the right people for the right jobs, be they internal or outsourced employees. You must establish a comprehensive investment policy statement ("IPS"). Next you have to figure out a legitimate measuring stick to understand what investment success will look like. Good governance means monitoring results, making changes when necessary or sitting on your hands and following your plan when that's the right course of action. The correct governance structure will account for the competency and skills of board and investment committee members.

And, just like builders, doctors and airline pilots, the institutional investor needs checklists of their own to ensure a well-functioning decision-making process is in place. However, it's worth pointing out that a checklist or documented investment process are not the be-all, end-all when making decisions. You have to understand where and when to use them correctly.

There are two types of checklists. The first is called a Read-Do checklist. This is where you would read instructions and check them off the list, following the instructions exactly as they are stated, just like a recipe from a cookbook. The second type is called a Do-Confirm checklist. This one offers more flexibility in performing your tasks, but you still have to stop when making key decisions to ensure that you've gone through your process correctly and discussed all of the variables involved. It allows you to make sure everything that is supposed to happen in your decision-making process does happen and no huge areas of concern are overlooked.

You have to pick the type of checklist that makes the most sense for the situation. The investment process will require some tasks in the Read-Do format, but most decisions will be made using a Do-Confirm format to allow for critical thinking during complex scenarios.

These are the basics for institutional investors:

- An Investment Policy Statement

- An Investment Committee Charter
- A Spending Policy Statement
- Cash Management Guidelines

I will go through each in the following section.

INVESTMENT POLICY STATEMENT

The IPS is your ultimate checklist as an organization. Without an IPS your investment program is like a rudderless ship that is likely to drift aimlessly because it has no established direction. An IPS is the document that lays out the purpose of the funds in question.

Every IPS will be different based on the unique needs and circumstances of the organization in question, but the following list will provide a good starting point for what should be included in a comprehensive plan:

- State the purpose of the document and the organization's mission.
- Lay out the goals and objectives for the fund.
- Define the role of the investment committee.
- Define the risk profile of the organization.
- Discuss how those objectives are going to become a reality.
- Define any spending or liquidity needs and constraints.
- State your investment philosophy.
- Spell out performance and risk expectations and targets.
- Define a benchmark portfolio (and make sure it's liquid and investable).
- List the policy portfolio or asset allocation targets for each asset class or investment style.
- Discuss the rebalancing policies and procedures.
- Be very specific about investment criteria in terms of guidelines, policies, restrictions and constraints.
- Clarify on the exact the types of assets, fund structures and investment styles the fund will and will not invest in.
- Lay out the various risk management and diversification policies.
- Determine when investment performance will be reviewed and spell out how investments will be evaluated.

I've seen many organizations who have an IPS in place but it's something they put together a number of years ago, never to be seen or heard from again. The point of reviewing the IPS on a periodic basis - say, once a year - is not to continually make changes to an investment program and portfolio. That would defeat the purpose. You should only make changes when necessary. The point of reviewing the IPS is to remind everyone involved why you're investing in the first place. If the document is set up correctly, going over it on an annual basis will be a great way to remind all parties involved what the original goals were to begin with. It can be a conversation starter - or conversation ender - depending on the current proposals. An IPS can also act as something of a benchmark to ensure that your investment program is successful or not.

INVESTMENT COMMITTEE CHARTER

Being a member of the Investment Committee is an important role because you act as something of a go-between for the rest of the organization and the investment funds. It's important for committee members to understand their roles within the construct of the fund and the organization. As we mentioned earlier in the book, the average tenure for a board member is relatively short. Having a document in place that describes what the job entails when a new trustee enters the board can help with the transition process and ensure current members know their role.

This is important because very few institutional Investment Committee members have professional investment experience. One study looked at nearly 900 trustees on various pension plans across the U.S. It discovered that only 23 percent of trustees had any experience in asset management while just 2 percent held the Chartered Financial Analyst (CFA) designation.

There's nothing wrong with having people outside the world of finance oversee the investments. In fact, it can be a benefit to have a diversity of opinions. But it then becomes very important for the Investment Committee to understand their roles and where they can or cannot add value. This is the point of the Investment Committee Charter. You want to have documentation in place, a regular meeting schedule, well-qualified and knowledgeable people and ensure that no conflicts of interest exist.

Here are some of the main points and/or tasks to consider for a useful Investment Committee Charter:

- Establish the purpose of the Investment Committee.
- Examine the makeup of the membership (number of people, tenure, etc.).
- Define and outline the various roles and responsibilities of the board members, investment committee members, consultants, advisors and money managers.

- Define how trustees can fulfill their fiduciary duty on behalf of the fund's beneficiaries and organizational mission.
- Lay out the frequency of investment meetings and reviews.
- Outline the duties, authorities and responsibilities for all those involved with the investment funds.
- Document compensation arrangements.
- Discuss expectations for future members.
- Determine how members of the Investment Committee are selected and who is to be Chair.
- Determine what reports the Board expects from the Investment Committee, and how often they are to receive these reports.
- Solidify which decisions of the Investment Committee must be ratified by the Board.
- Create a payout policy for the Fund that meets the organization's needs.

There should also be an understanding about the structure of the periodic meetings and what is expected to be covered on a regular basis. At least once a year there should be a review of the portfolio, organizational needs, goals, IPS, liquidity profile, procedures and costs. You don't want to get in the habit of simply reviewing the most recent performance numbers. You want the focus to be policy - fees, asset allocation, process, planning, risk management and communications - not short-term market events.

Investment committee meetings really shouldn't take all that long. You discuss the progress towards your goals and go over any changes organizational structure or needs. If not, re-state your goals, discuss your investment philosophy and figure out if there are any legitimate reasons to make changes to your portfolio that fall outside of your current plan and policy guidelines. The majority of the time there should be no changes made, assuming you have done the requisite upfront work and planning. You simply follow the agreed-upon decision-making process. Committees should spend the vast majority of their time on important topics that require them to think in terms of probabilities and outcomes. You should talk to your money managers, consultants or advisors at least once a year for these meetings, but anyone you're outsourcing for asset management purposes should be communicating with you in-between these meetings with periodic letters and conference calls anyways.

It's also critical for the Investment Committee to remind all involved with the portfolio the importance of long-term thinking and admitting their limitations. In an interview with financial writer Jason Zweig, Charles Ellis, who you've met throughout these chapters, describes how a successful long-term investor should think much like a tree farmer over time:

If you ran a commercial tree farm, would you ask for up-to-the-minute bulletins on how the forest was growing today? How many people are investing for success this year, this month, this week, this day? Most people's true time horizons are much longer than they think - 50 years, even more. They should be investing for success over a lifetime - or more than one lifetime, because part of what they're investing will go to their kids after they're gone.

When given enough water, light, air and space a tree can grow to great heights as long as you pretty much leave it alone. The same is true of a well-constructed portfolio.

SPENDING POLICY STATEMENT

The long-term is the only time frame that truly matters but nonprofits still have to be able to survive the short-term and meet their operating needs. That's the entire point of the funds, after all. Plenty of organizations learned this lesson the hard way during the Great Financial Crisis of 2007-2009. A number of both large and small institutions ran into a liquidity or funding crisis during this period because they didn't really understand the risks involved in the financial markets. Many didn't have contingency plans in place and were forced to cut back on spending, let go of employees or even close their doors.

This is where the importance of a comprehensive investment plan really earns its stripes. Anyone can invest successfully when things are going well. But when things turn ugly, that's where you really discover where a true process and plan are in place. The Spending Policy Statement can play a huge part in surviving these downturns.

Just as there are no perfect investment portfolios, there are also no perfect spending policies. Every policy will require some trade-offs between current and future spending needs. Higher expected returns lead to more short-term volatility, while predictable spending patterns tend to accompany lower expected returns. That means you have to consider spending goals in terms of the current market value of the portfolio along with the sensitivity to past market values and spending levels.

Spending rules are meant to help deal with the trade-off between the desire for long-term capital preservation and short-term spending smoothness. The type of fund can have a lot to do with figuring out where to begin with this process. Here are some considerations for the various types of institutional funds:

Pensions. Pensions typically have the least amount of flexibility with their investment approach because they have a defined liability - future or current payouts to their beneficiaries. Pensions can thus match their assets with their liabilities when creating a portfolio. That's not always an easy task - especially with interest rates nearly on the floor at the moment - because any time you're dealing with risk assets you can't predict what's going to happen with any certainty. Pensions can calculate their funded status to determine the amount of risk they can or should take along with any need for additional contributions to the plan. With a large number of underfunded plans this will be something worth paying attention to in the years ahead as millions of baby boomers continue to retire.

Foundations. Charitable foundations have more investment flexibility but many have to make a minimum payout of 5 percent of their assets each year to support charitable purposes or face tax penalties. Typically, this means that foundations will have lower risk profiles than endowments, but higher risk profiles than pensions. There are a number of unique variables that can determine where each fund risk profile ends up depending on the unique circumstances involved, such as the amount of charitable donations brought in. However, most foundations rely heavily on investment returns to meet spending needs. In 2006, 8 of the 10 largest grant-making foundations received almost 100 percent of their total revenues from investment portfolios.

Endowments. Endowments have a general lack of constraints on investment and spending needs so they have greater flexibility than either pensions or foundations. Not only do they have longer time horizons, but many college endowments, particularly large funds, enjoy gifts from alumni which decreases the need to spend from the investment portfolio. Endowments and foundations are both generally looking to balance out competing goals: preserving their long-term purchasing power against the ability to plan for a smooth payout policy.

There are a number of variables that will affect an organization's spending policy and payout:

- Contributions, distributions, and investment earnings.
- Liquidity preferences and needs.
- Asset allocation decisions.
- Available resources.
- Percentage of the overall operating budget that comes from investments.
- The timing of cash flows.
- Spending requirements.

- Actual vs. expected returns.
- Cash reserves.

Donations are always a good problem to have but they can be hard to plan for because they tend to ebb and flow with the economic and market cycles. It's difficult to rely on gifts as a hedge against a stock market crash because those are the times when charitable donations tend to dry up. And the closer your expected return number is to your expected spending rate, the harder it is to stay consistent with your spending levels because you don't leave the fund with a huge margin for error. All of these variables must be considered when selecting the policy that works for your particular fund.

A few examples can be helpful to consider how most institutions handle their spending policies in the real world:

1. Percentage-of-Assets Spending Rate. This policy would simply use a fixed percentage (say 5 percent of total assets) and grow it by the rate of inflation each year.

Pros: It's a simple policy.
Cons: Your spending amount will vary considerably if you have a portfolio invested in risk assets.

2. Smoothed or Moving-Average Spending Rate. To smooth out the potential volatility in the annual payout many funds utilize a moving average. For example, you could take the average of the previous three or five years' spending amounts to determine your current spending amount or rate.

Pros: Less variable than a flat rate and a relatively simple policy.
Cons: Current year spending could be determined by stale values in the past that don't reflect new organizational or market realities.

3. Hybrid Spending Rate. This is a combination of the first two where you could use a partial dollar amount grown by inflation and a partial smoothing factor. You could also add a ceiling and a floor to keep things in line and not go too high or too low when times are either wonderful or horrible in the markets. Swensen says that Yale's endowment utilizes a hybrid approach that's equal to 80 percent of spending in the previous year plus 20 percent of the long-term spending rate.

Pros: Reduces the impact of volatile investments on current spending.
Cons: Introduces more complexity into the equation when trying to balance

the current and past values.

According to one study, up to 75 percent of institutions use a smoothing policy, with over 70 percent of institutions ending up spending somewhere in the 4 percent to 6 percent range in terms of their current market values. Regardless of the spending policy chosen, you have to learn to accept the tradeoffs involved and understand the volatility characteristics of your asset mix. Higher expected returns come from higher expected volatility. Introducing higher allocations to stocks should lead to higher expected long-term returns, but also more variability in short-term market values. That means you should expect a higher probability of preserving capital over the long-term, but also a higher probability of seeing large swings in your spending rates when using a simple percentage of assets approach.

Policies should guide your actions but flexibility will likely be a key component when trying to plan organizationally. Spending policies can't be completely controlled by the volatility of the portfolio but it can't be completely ignored either. A prudent plan would create reserves in good times to help during the times when markets are down.

There's no one-size-fits-all spending policy that will work for every fund or organization. The best policy will take into account what is most important for the institution in question. The constant tug-of-war between current and future spending needs must be hashed out when thinking through this decision. The right spending policy will be the one that is able to balance out these two competing initiatives.

CASH MANAGEMENT GUIDELINES

Once you have your spending policies in place you have to actually figure out how to manage your liquidity. Cash management is an often overlooked aspect in all of this. That money has to be there when you need to spend it. They say liquidity is like oxygen – you don't notice it until you need it and it's not there. The goal should always be to ensure that you can meet your short-term spending distributions with as little risk as possible. There are places to take risk and there are places to avoid risk. Cash management is one of the places in which you should be looking to avoid taking on too much risk.

Here are some considerations when thinking about cash management:

- The size of the portfolio allocation to cash or cash equivalents that are bookmarked for spending purposes.
- Banking services and fees.
- Safety of principal.

- Liquidity needs and timelines.
- The desire or need for current returns.
- The acceptable level of risk.

I've seen some organizations who want 1-2 years' worth of spending cash in ultra safe holdings; for others it could be 1-3 months. Some organizations use their rebalancing proceeds to fund current payouts while others have the luxury of using donations or gifts. This is another decision that comes down to knowing and understanding your own personal needs and tolerance for risk. Some organizations are very conservative while others want every last cent to be fully invested for as long as possible. Investing is a form of regret minimization so there needs to be a balance in place.

You'll notice that each of these policies eventually comes down to trade-offs. As they say, investing is simple but never easy.

PEOPLE

Policies and documentation are important to set the tone for the organization, but it won't matter if you don't have the right people in place who can implement it in real time when things don't go as planned. Planning should be the easy part. The implementation, monitoring, course corrections and plan changes (when necessary) are what separates successful organizations from everyone else. Everyone needs to be on the same page - leadership, board members, the investment committee, advisors, consultants, money managers, etc.

In my experience, the best people are honest, transparent, ask for help when they need it, know what they don't know, know how to communicate effectively, admit their mistakes and are generally easy to work with.

Here's how David Swensen describes a successful board, which should work for everyone involved in the process:

> *Competent boards have a preponderance of people of character who are comfortable doing their organizational thinking in multi-year time frames. These people understand ambiguity and uncertainty, and are still prepared to go ahead and make the required judgments and decisions. They know what they don't know.*

Charley Ellis described three characteristics of a successful investment organization in a recent talk (which I am paraphrasing for brevity):

1. They make sure they spend enough time on the big decisions.
2. They have a tremendous consistency on their basic values or philosophy.

3. They have great clients and work with high caliber people.

Thinking in these terms is one of reasons Yale's endowment has been so successful over the years. Even the best investment policies in the world won't matter all that much if you don't have the right people implementing them.

CONCLUSION: CREATING ORGANIZATIONAL ALPHA

During World War II the U.S. manufactured nearly 300,000 aircrafts. Airplanes were still a relatively new technology and weapon at the time. They were also expensive. The majority of the bombings missions were carried out by B-17s, which cost in upwards of $200,000 to make (close to $3 million in today's dollars). To state the obvious, the missions these planes were being used for in the war were dangerous. Over the course of the WWII, there were almost 50,000 planes that went missing or got shot down.

Thus, the engineers of these planes spent a lot of time figuring out how to add extra protection to the planes to ensure a safe return home for the pilots. So they began studying the planes that did make it back from battle by examining where the bullet holes were. The thinking was that it made sense to shore up these areas of the planes by adding more armor since that's where the enemies were causing damage. This would make intuitive sense, but they were actually looking at this problem all wrong.

A mathematician named Abraham Wald started thinking about this problem by using a diagram of the planes to mark the spots where they were being shot at. Bullet holes littered the various planes save for a few crucial spots. So Wald started to look at the problem backwards - he inverted it by looking where the planes had not been hit. The planes that were returning to base were the ones who didn't get shot down. Yes, they got shot, but the spots they were being hit didn't take them down or disable their flight capabilities. Thus, Wald determined that the planes that were being shot down and not returning were getting hit in crucial areas outside of these regions. He determined that the vulnerable locations on the plane were by the fuel tanks and cockpit so it made sense to protect those areas with more armor, not the spots where the returning planes were getting hit. They obviously couldn't study the planes that had been shot down so they were looking at this problem all wrong. This helped the manufacturers of these planes armor them in the spots that could actually protect the pilots in the future.

Most businesses, organizations and investors are always looking for success stories to emulate. And I understand why this happens. There's nothing wrong with standing on the shoulder of giants. But very few look in the other direction by studying companies, strategies, organizations or investors who have failed trying a similar approach. The winners write the history books, but the greatest lessons from history tend to come from the losers. An intelligent organization will recognize their strengths, but a wise one will understand their weaknesses and limitations.

For example, State Street performed a survey of a wide variety of institutional investors ranging from sovereign wealth funds to endowments and foundations to insurance and pension plans. There were over 400 funds in the study, the majority of which managed billions of dollars. When asked for their five-year expected forward returns in 2015, here is what this group came up with by asset class and in total:

Asset Class	Return Expectations
Stocks	10.0%
Bonds	5.5%
Commodities	8.9%
Real Estate	10.9%
Total Portfolio	**10.9%**

Mind you, this is following one of the greatest bull markets in history over the previous six plus years, yet these investors are all deluding themselves into believing that they will hit the ball out of the park. Not only will it be difficult for these institutions to see these types of returns over the next five years, but very few of them were able to achieve this kind of performance over the previous five years, when valuations were much lower and interest rates were slightly higher.

Now, take a look at how impatient this group can be with their investments when asked how long they would stick with active managers or smart beta funds following periods of underperformance:

How long is underperformance tolerated before seeking a replacement?

Active Managers			Smart Beta Managers		
40%	49%	11%	80%	19%	1%
1 Year	2 Years	3 Years	1 Year	2 Years	3 Years

Source: State Street

According to this survey, 90 percent of these institutional investors give their investments just two years or less before cutting them loose and moving on to the new flavor of the month. This is madness and provides a nice explanation for the persistent performance chase and poor returns that so many institutional investors are dealing with.

Another study from Greenwich Associates asked institutional investors - endowments, corporate funds, pension plans, etc. - what their performance expectations were for the money managers they invested with. On average, this group expected their funds to outperform the averages by 1 percent per year. There are well over 1,000 pension and endowment funds who collectively oversee these money managers so it's a statistical impossibility that they could all outperform the market by 100 basis points a year. The reason so many investors see below-average results is because they assume they're above average investors.

In an effort to be or beat the best, many investors end up being their own worst enemies. Simply avoiding these types of mistakes can make a huge difference to your bottom line.

Avoiding stupidity is much easier than emulating brilliance. You have to do the right things in order to succeed, but most people don't try to accomplish that by avoiding the huge mistakes. This is what organizational alpha is all about and it's how smaller and mid-sized institutions can achieve better results than those institutional investors who are managing billions of dollars.

To summarize, these are the main tenets of organizational alpha:

- Think in terms of process over outcomes.
- Know thyself when creating your investment and decision-making processes.
- Diagnose your problems before prescribing solutions.
- Be stubborn on your overall philosophy but flexible on the details.
- Document your investment process to cut down on unnecessary mistakes.
- Make decisions that revolve around the goals and mission of the organization.
- Understand and define everyone's roles.
- Ask yourself what future events could cause your plan to turn south.
- Understand what could happen if and when things go wrong.
- Always keep in mind your risk profile and time horizon when making investment decisions.
- Set realistic expectations with the understanding that the future is always uncertain.
- Always leave a margin of safety, since no one gets everything right.
- Know that managing money successfully is simple, but not easy.
- Always think in terms of trade-offs when making decisions.

- Focus on what you control.

There's never been a time when this has been more important to your bottom line as an institutional investor. Interest rates are near record lows. The funded status for pension plans looks to only get worse in the coming years. Not only is there more competition for alpha in the markets, but there's never been higher competition for charitable dollars, as well. Nonprofits are going to have an increasingly difficult time finding consistent sources of funding for all of the charitable work they would like to accomplish. The need for clear, level-headed, common sense decision-making has never been higher.

In closing, here are a few more questions to ask yourself as an organization:

What are we trying to accomplish?

What are our core beliefs?

Do we have the structures and processes in place to act on those beliefs?

Why are we trying to do this?

How are we going to get from here to there?

ABOUT THE AUTHOR

Ben Carlson, CFA is the Director of Institutional Asset Management at Ritholtz Wealth Management. He has spent his career working with various nonprofit, institutional and high net worth clients to help them plan and invest their money wisely. He is the author of the book *A Wealth of Common Sense: Why Simplicity Trumps Complexity in Any Investment Plan* and is the author of the blog, A Wealth of Common Sense.

REFERENCES

Introduction
Pioneering Portfolio Management: An Unconventional Approach to
Institutional Management. David Swensen. Simon & Schuster. 2009.

"Key Facts on U.S. Foundations: 2014 Edition." Foundation Center.
www.foundationcenter.org

NACUBO-CommonFund Study of Endowments: 2015. National
Association of College and University Business Officers.
http://www.nacubo.org/Research/NACUBO-
Commonfund_Study_of_Endowments.html

The Institutional ETF Toolbox. Eric Balchunas. John Wiley & Sons and
Bloomberg Press. 2016.

Chapter 1
"A Fireside Chat With Charlie Munger." Jason Zweig. The Wall Street
Journal. September 2014.
http://blogs.wsj.com/moneybeat/2014/09/12/a-fireside-chat-with-charlie-
munger/

"The Biggest Threat to Your Portfolio (It's Not What You Think). Motley
Fool. Morgan Housel. January 2013.
http://www.fool.com/investing/general/2013/01/25/the-biggest-threat-
to-your-portfolio-its-not-what.aspx

Pioneering Portfolio Management: An Unconventional Approach to
Institutional Management. David Swensen. Simon & Schuster. 2009.

Chapter 2
"The Wall Street Golden Boy Who Allegedly Fleeced His Friends and
Family." William D. Cohan. Vanity Fair. Summer 2016.
http://www.vanityfair.com/news/2016/06/andrew-caspersen-fraud

Pioneering Portfolio Management: An Unconventional Approach to
Institutional Management. David Swensen. Simon & Schuster. 2009.

Chapter 3
Winning the Loser's Game: Timeless Strategies for Successful Investing.
Charles D. Ellis. McGraw Hill. 2010.

Charlie Munger: The Complete Investor. Columbia Business School. Tren Griffin. 2015

Influence: The Psychology of Persuasion. Robert B. Cialdini, Ph.D. 1984. HarperCollins.
PERSI video

Asch, S.E. (1951). Effects of group pressure on the modification and distortion of judgments. In H. Guetzkow (Ed.), Groups, leadership and men(pp. 177–190). Pittsburgh, PA:Carnegie Press.

PERSI Chief Investment Officer Bob Maynard presents "Conventional Investing in a Complex World"
https://www.youtube.com/watch?v=_rrnPWekNYU August 2013.

"Theory-Driven Reasoning About Plausible Pasts and Probable Futures in World Politics: Are We Prisoners of Our Preconceptions?" Philip E. Tetlock. American Journal of Political Science, Vol. 43, No. 2 (Apr. 1999), 335-366.

The Power of Habit: Why We Do What We Do In Life and Business. Charles Duhigg. Random House. 2012.

Pioneering Portfolio Management: An Unconventional Approach to Institutional Management. David Swensen. Simon & Schuster. 2009.

Chapter 4
"Pete Carroll Inspires the Armed Forces." Ben Malcolmson. June 2009. USC News. https://news.usc.edu/27309/pete-carroll-inspires-the-armed-forces/

The Incredible Shrinking Alpha: And What You Can Do to Escape Its Clutches. Larry Swedroe and Andrew Berkin. BAM Alliance Press. January 2015.

"Spotting the Next Superstar Fund Manager." Steven Goldberg. Kiplinger. June 2013. http://m.kiplinger.com/article/investing/T041-C007-S003-spotting-the-next-superstar-fund-manager.html

Dear Chairman: Boardroom Battles and the Rise of Shareholder Activism. Jeff Gramm. 2015. Harper Collins.

Skating Where the Puck Was: The Correlation Game in a Flat World. William Bernstein. 2012. Amazon Digital Services LLC.

"The Selection and Termination of Investment Management Firms by Plan Sponsors." Amit Goyal, Sunil Wahal. The Journal of Finance, Vol. 63, Issue 4, August 2008.

Unconventional Success: A Fundamental Approach to Personal Investment. David Swensen. Simon & Schuster. 2005.

NACUBO-CommonFund Study of Endowments: 2015. National Association of College and University Business Officers. http://www.nacubo.org/Research/NACUBO-Commonfund_Study_of_Endowments.html

Pioneering Portfolio Management: An Unconventional Approach to Institutional Management. David Swensen. Simon & Schuster. 2009.

Chapter 5
Thinking, Fast & Slow. Daniel Kahneman. Farrar, Straus and Giroux. 2011.

Scott D. Stewart, John J. Neumann, Christopher R. Knittel, & Jeffrey Heisler, "Absence of Value: An Analysis of Investment Allocation Decisions by Institutional Plan Sponsors," Financial Analysts Journal 65, no. 6 (2009).

Andrew Ang, Amit Goyal, & Antii Ilmanen, "Asset Allocation and Bad Habits," April 2014

2015 Berkshire Hathaway Annual Meeting. Omaha, Nebraska

Pioneering Portfolio Management: An Unconventional Approach to Institutional Management. David Swensen. Simon & Schuster. 2009.

Chapter 6
Hedge Funds Provide Worst Long-Term Gains to Pension Plans. Bloomberg. July 2016. John Gittelsohn. http://www.bloomberg.com/news/articles/2016-07-01/hedge-funds-provide-worst-long-term-gains-to-u-s-pension-plans

"Consultant: Hedge Funds 'Integral' to Corporate Pensions." Amy Whyte. Chief Investment Officer. June 2016. http://www.ai-cio.com/channel/Manager-Selection/Consultant--Hedge-Funds--Integral--

to-Corporate-Pensions/

Securities and Exchange Commission. Division of Investment Management: Risk and Examinations Office. Private Fund Statistics Fourth Calendar Quarter 2014. https://www.sec.gov/divisions/investment/private-funds-statistics/private-funds-statistics-2014-q4.pdf

The Hedge Fund Mirage: The Illusion of Big Money and Why It's Too Good to Be True. Simon Lack. 2011. John Wiley & Sons.

Unconventional Success: A Fundamental Approach to Personal Investment. David Swensen. Simon & Schuster. 2005.

The Yale (and Harvard, Stanford, MIT.) Model. Chief Investment Officer. Sage Um. May 2016. http://www.ai-cio.com/channel/ASSET-ALLOCATION/The-Yale-(and-Harvard,-Stanford,-MIT---)-Model/

Pioneering Portfolio Management: An Unconventional Approach to Institutional Management. David Swensen. Simon & Schuster. 2009.

Chapter 7
A Look at the U.S. Commercial Building Stock: Results from EIA's 2012 Commercial Buildings Energy Consumption Survey (CBECS). March 2015. https://www.eia.gov/consumption/commercial/reports/2012/buildstock/

The Checklist Manifesto: How to Get Things Right. Atul Gawande. 2010. Metropolitan Books.

"Wall Street's Wisest Man." Money Magazine. Jason Zweig. June 2001.

"Swedroe: When Board Members Hurt Returns." Larry Swedroe. ETF.com. June 2016. http://www.etf.com/sections/index-investor-corner/swedroe-when-board-members-hurt-returns?nopaging=1

"Risk-Return Tradeoffs in Endowment Spending and Portfolio Policies." Massi De Santis. Dimensional Fund Advisors. January 2014.

"The Characteristics of Successful Investment Firms." Charles D. Ellis. Managing the Investment Professional. September 1983. http://www.cfapubs.org/doi/pdf/10.2469/cp.v1984.n1.5

Pioneering Portfolio Management: An Unconventional Approach to Institutional Management. David Swensen. Simon & Schuster. 2009.

Conclusion
WWII Aircraft Facts. WWII Foundation.
http://www.wwiifoundation.org/students/wwii-aircraft-facts/

"Invert, always invert." Robert Seawright. Above the Market. December 2013. https://rpseawright.wordpress.com/2013/12/17/invert-always-invert/

The Index Revolution: Why Investors Should Join It Now. Charles D. Ellis. John Wiley & Sons. September 2016.

Made in the USA
San Bernardino, CA
07 February 2017